BATTING

HOW TO PLAY, COACH AND WIN

BATTING

HOW TO PLAY, COACH AND WIN

**Mark Davis
and Sam Collins**

Published in the UK in 2012 by
John Wisden & Co.
An imprint of Bloomsbury Publishing Plc
50 Bedford Square, London WC1B 3DP
www.wisden.com
www.bloomsbury.com

ISBN 978 1 4081 4654 5

Guidance on the wearing of helmets (page 18) and modes of dismissal (pages 128–9)
reproduced by permission of the England and Wales Cricket Board.

A CIP catalogue record for this book is available from the British Library.

Designed by Greg Stevenson
Cover photograph © Getty Images
Photographs on pages xi, 39, 51, 55, 59, 63, 66, 67, 72, 78, 82, 84, 88, 92, 103, 109,
114, 116, 118 and 120 © Getty Images
All other photographs © Grant Pritchard
Illustrations by Greg Stevenson

This book is produced using paper that is made from wood grown in managed,
sustainable forests. It is natural, renewable and recyclable. The logging and
manufacturing processes conform to the environmental regulations of the country
of origin.

Typeset in 11 point Joanna by Saxon Graphics Ltd, Derby
Printed and bound in Great Britain by Clays Ltd, St Ives plc

CONTENTS

FOREWORD

Not one single batsman in the world has a perfect technique. The search for that perfect technique is the crux of everything a batsman does, but no one will ever get it – it's impossible to hit every ball in the middle of the bat. That's what's great about cricket – every batsman is human and we all have flaws. A batsman's skill lies in how they acknowledge, understand and deal with those flaws.

I remember scoring my first hundred on my eleventh birthday. Then it was all about that amazing feeling of emulating the heroes that I'd watched on the television. The higher up you go, the more recognition you get for those hundreds. Going to county and international cricket the roar from the crowd when you hit a boundary or score a century is addictive, and it's those moments that get you through the low times.

Yet the higher you get, the more complicated things can become, and the more advice you will be given. When you're going through a rough patch and you're sifting through that advice, the hardest thing to do can be to remember the simplicity of the game.

When anyone starts playing cricket it's just about trying to whack the red thing as far as possible and having fun doing it. That forms the basis of batting really – watch the ball and hit it. People make it more complicated than that, but it doesn't have to be. The biggest thing is to have fun, otherwise there's no point in doing it.

Of all the things I've learned at this early stage in my career, three things stand out. Graham Gooch said something to me when I was opening the batting at the World Twenty20 in 2010 that has stuck with me. He told me there is a difference between the art of batting and the art of scoring runs, and the art of scoring runs is more important. It's not how you get them it's how many.

While I am known as a stroke-maker, Graham Thorpe taught me a valuable lesson about the uglier side of batting. Batting is just as much about hanging in there when things aren't going your way. At those times it's about always working hard to get to the other end. Instead of trying to hit every ball for four, sometimes it's more important to get to the non-striker's end and take stock again. A single can be just as important as a boundary.

Finally, I remember playing against Lancashire in my debut season, and they had a brilliant bowling attack – Andrew Flintoff, James Anderson, Saj Mahmood and Glenn Chapple – all England internationals. I was a bit overawed

at the prospect of Freddie (Flintoff) running in at me, but Justin Langer (who was playing with us at the time) told me to imagine I was playing a club game, and to concentrate on the ball not the bowler. His point was that momentum is always shifting between batsman and bowler in cricket, no matter how good the bowler you are playing against is, but you have to convince yourself you can score runs against any bowler.

Above all, remember to respect and enjoy the game.

I got to know Mark Davis very well when I came across to Millfield School. He was probably the first coach that helped me to develop my game. We did a lot of hard work in the winter in the indoor school and he was very generous with his advice and the dedication that he showed towards helping me to develop as a cricketer. He gave me my first real chance by getting me the trial that got me my contract at Somerset, and from there I haven't looked back. I owe a lot to Mark because without him I might not be playing international cricket today.

CRAIG KIESWETTER (MILLFIELD, SOMERSET AND ENGLAND),
SEPTEMBER 2011

INTRODUCTION

Batting is a major trial before an 11-man jury.
RICHIE BENAUD, AUSTRALIAN CAPTAIN

Cricket is constantly changing. Ten years ago Twenty20 didn't even exist, now it sets the international agenda. With the changes come the new shots, the new deliveries, the fads. Ten years ago some of the shots in this book would not have featured, some had not even been invented. In ten years' time everybody may be playing them, or they may have been forgotten. That is change.

If a batsman wants to know what they should take from this book, or any coaching textbook, they should look at the English batsmen Alastair Cook, Ian Bell, Kevin Pietersen and Eoin Morgan as proof that the answer is everything and nothing. Cook and Bell are textbook run-scorers of every era, system-nurtured batsmen of very different techniques that meet in the middle at their orthodoxy. In contrast Pietersen and Morgan are the two most exciting developments in the recent history of English batting yet are coaching book mongrels, men who have walked their own path, made their own systems, and developed their own very unorthodox styles. One of Morgan's former coaches told me last year that he had only had the freedom to develop an individual technique because he was brought up away from the strait-jacketing of ECB academies.

The best thing about those four batsmen is that they show better than any book that there is no right way or wrong way to bat. All four have scored centuries in limited-over formats and Test cricket for England. Good players can score runs in any form of the game. As to which type a batsman might want to copy, if at all, that's their call. Whatever the build, the personality, or the type of game a batsman might already have there is hope.

Coaching books can sound so definitive: 'Do this or else.' Sometimes that's true, but largely it's not. This book, and any other coaching book, is just a framework. This book gives suggestions that a batsman might want to follow. It is there to enthuse, to fire the imagination, to start the thought process about which shots are still to be mastered. The main aim is to help each batsman understand their own technique.

THE BASICS

1.

THE SET-UP

Before we get on to the shots it's important to start at the basics of any batsman's technique – the **grip**, the **stance**, **back-lift**, **taking guard** and **trigger movements**. These comprise the batsman's **set-up**, and if a batsman ever wants to smash a quick bowler through the covers or play the perfect reverse-sweep, they'll need to get these right first.

Patience is key when working on these skills. The batsman may find them difficult to master straight away, but it'll be worth it in the long run.

This may be step one of lesson one in batting, but don't underestimate its importance. It is surprising how many of the technical problems a batsman may experience down the line can be fixed simply by going back and following these set-up basics.

It's also important to remember that every batsman might have a slightly different set-up. That is no bad thing, as long as the basic principles are adhered to. A good set-up should ensure the batsman is balanced and comfortable at the crease, can see the ball correctly, and their bat is coming down in a straight line. Beyond these key principles the batsman should **do whatever works for them**.

The grip
What it is

Before doing anything, a batsman has got to know how to hold the bat correctly. The right grip is vital to give control of the bat and power in the shot, not to mention making sure that the ball goes where the batsman intends it to. A good grip ensures that the bat comes down straight to meet the ball – the basis for all the shots the batsman will learn about.

There are two main types of grip – the 'Vs' grip, and the 'O' grip. Once the batsman is happy and confident with these basic grips, they can adapt the grip to suit their game or particular challenges they might face, but are advised to remember that **a grip should allow them to swing the bat in a straight line in a pendulum motion**.

However the batsman holds the bat, they shouldn't squeeze it too hard. The top hand should be the dominant hand, gripping the bat firmly, while the bottom hand acts as support. The batsman's arms should feel relaxed.

The 'Vs' grip
How to do it

- Place hands together on the bat handle with two 'Vs' created by the shape of fore finger and thumb. Both 'Vs' should line up between the splice of the bat and the outside edge.

- The top hand should be about an inch from the top of the bat with equal pressure by the hands on the bat. The back of the top hand should be facing between mid-off and extra cover.

- The top hand is in control of the pick-up. It is essential that the bat path swings like the pendulum of a clock. The top hand is in control and the bottom hand acts as a support.

- Some players operate a simple 'two finger and thumb' grip, where this lighter grip with the bottom hand sees it act merely as a support. As the shot is played, the bottom hand is engaged fully into the shot.

Practice drill

- Simple techniques are to place the bat on the ground and pick it up naturally with both hands together. The batsman should line up the two 'Vs' or place the bat on the front thigh and repeat the process.

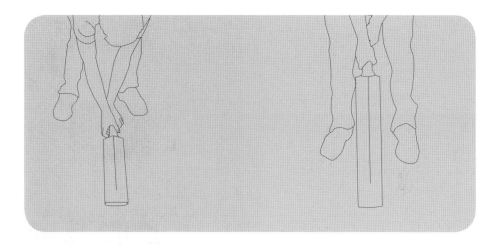

The 'O' grip

What it is

As batsmen develop, some tend to find the traditional 'Vs' grip is not powerful enough. They will then slip into an 'O' grip. The 'O' grip is good for improving general back foot play, i.e. pull shot, back foot punches. However, it can be restrictive when driving through extra cover, or playing square of the wicket off the back foot. There are notable exponents of the 'O' grip including the South African opener Graeme Smith, but young players should be wary of the limitations it imposes at a young age.

How to do it

- The 'O' grip is where the right hand slides down to the bottom of the bat with the fingers wrapped around the bat. This often happens if the bat is too heavy or the player is searching for extra power in the shot.

Problems and fixes

- *Bottom hand becomes too dominant and goes round in the grip.* Maintain the strength in the top hand.

- *Bat face closes on impact with the ball.* Release the grip with the bottom hand and allow the top hand and the front elbow to be dominant. The top hand and the front elbow is the guider, and the bottom hand is the enforcer – one can't work without the other.

The stance

What it is

A comfortable base is essential for any batsman – batting is hard work and it's important for the batsman to be as relaxed as possible. The stance should keep the batsman's head and eyes level and looking at the bowler, and enable them to move backwards and forwards in the crease as quickly and as easily as possible.

How to do it

- Start with feet about shoulder-width apart and parallel to the crease. Knees should be slightly bent and relaxed. Draw an imaginary line down from the groin – the head should not push level or beyond the front foot, or go over the balls of the feet to the offside. Done correctly this will give the batsman the balance required to access all areas of the crease.

  N.B. The batsman must keep his foot or bat grounded behind the line of the batting crease.

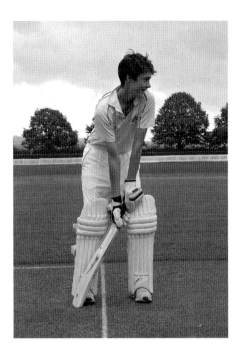

- The batsman's heel and toe should have contact with the ground, while head and eyes should be in line with the balls of the feet.

- The batsman should place the bat behind the back foot, and tap the bat to the ground as many times as feels comfortable. When the bowler is in the take-off 'bound' position, pick up the bat by bending the front elbow and taking the hands back, level to the back pocket. The bat height should be ¾ to stump height. The batsman should be light on their feet and ready to move quickly into position.

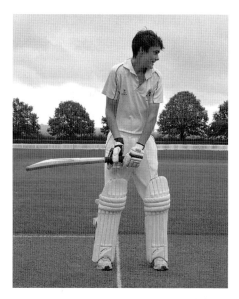

Your eyes should be level at all times, especially when the ball is released. Line up your eyes with the top of the grille on your helmet. Try to focus on the ball when the bowler jumps into his delivery position. Once you decide what length the ball is, you can then move your head into position. The hands and body follow before the shot is played.

Widening of the base

- Some players prefer a wider stance. This could be wider than shoulder-width apart. From this position, footwork is kept to a minimum. A famous example is the Somerset and former England batsman Marcus Trescothick.

- This stance is usually employed by batsmen who are unable to stop their head from moving as the ball is released. With practice, it can be very effective.

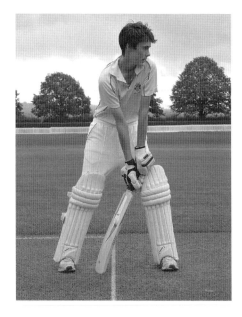

- Due to the widening of the base, the bat will now be placed in the centre of the stance, not behind as with a conventional stance. The wider stance is more about transferring weight into the shot either forward or back.

- The **positives** of this stance are that the timing and power of the shot are much improved – merely a left-shoulder dip into the drives or a rock-back when the ball is short.

- A **negative** aspect is that the bat can be drawn away from the body. This can cause the bat face to close. The stance also impedes quick feet, meaning it is difficult for the batsman to get down the wicket quickly to spin.

EXPERT COACHING TIP

This is useful for a quick fix, for example for a young batsman who has just gone into a growth spurt and lost their balance. After a period of time, the batsman should be encouraged to return to a more orthodox stance.

Open stance
- Some batsmen like to use a more open stance. Rather than aligning the shoulders straight back down the wicket, the batsman opens their stance so that the shoulders line up with the slip cordon instead.

- The open stance might be adopted because the batsman has one eye dominant over the other, or because they are struggling with their leg-side play. On a **positive** note the opening of the stance can make the batsman feel more balanced and improve leg-side play. It can also be useful if facing a left-arm over the wicket bowler, as the batsman is lined up more to the line of the bowler.

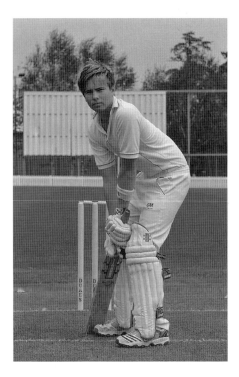

- A **negative** with the open stance is that it can make the batsman very susceptible to the out-swing bowler, as it is hard for the batsman to get their front foot outside off-stump, and they can end up playing away from their body.

Practice drill

- The batsman should stand in front of a full-length mirror with their eyes closed, without the bat, and stand in a relaxed, comfortable position with their feet shoulder-width apart and their knees slightly flexed. This is a good base from which to form the stance at the crease. Opening their eyes, the batsman can then go through a range of shots and examine in more detail the movements required.

Problems and fixes

- *Batsman's head falling to the off-side.* The batsman is overbalanced. The batsman's weight should be evenly distributed, with heel and toe in contact with the ground, but the weight on the balls of the feet. Eyes should be level, looking back up the pitch.

- *Stance gets too closed off.* This happens when the batsman's left shoulder is too far round, facing mid-off. It's impossible then not to pick the bat up to the leg side, and it leaves the batsman playing around his pads.

- *Stance gets too narrow.* Make sure the batsman is comfortable in the stance, and that the feet aren't too close together. Knees should be comfortable and flexed.

Nerves play as important a part in batsmanship as skill.
GILBERT JESSOP

The guard
What it is
The purpose of the batsman taking guard is to know where the off-stump is. It enables them to judge what line the ball is coming on, so they know which balls to leave alone, and which to play. Most batsmen tend to take a middle-stump, middle-and-leg or leg-stump guard, depending on where they like the off-stump to be in relation to their head position.

How to do it
- It is important for the batsman to understand their own strengths and weaknesses when thinking about taking guard.
- Strong off-side players often take a **leg-stump guard** as this encourages the bowler to bowl at the stumps, allowing the batter to free their arms and play to their strengths.
- **Middle-and-leg guard** allows the batsman to have their eyes level with the off-stump and so be in a better position to judge what shot to play. It also opens up the leg-side.
- **Middle or even middle-and-off-stump guard** suggests a strong leg-sided player. The batsman's eyes are outside off-stump, making it easier to leave balls alone. However, if the batsman misses, the bowler will get them either LBW or 'bowled' around their pads.

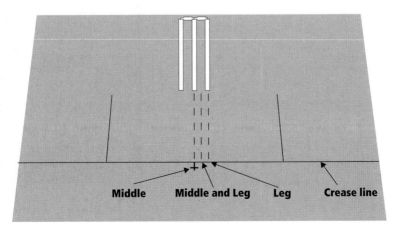

Middle   Middle and Leg   Leg   Crease line

If you have a trigger movement routine, this should be factored into the guard you take.

Practice drill

- The coach throws balls at the batsman on or around off-stump. The batsman is only allowed to play at balls they think are in line with the stumps. The batsman must tell the coach how far outside the off-stump the balls that they have left are. The coach should their give them feedback on how correct their perception of off-stump's position is. This will help the batsman to gain a better understanding of what balls they can or can't leave alone.

Problems and fixes

- *Keep being bowled leaving balls alone.* The batsman should examine their guard. If they are taking a leg-stump guard, move to a middle-stump guard.

Trigger movement

What it is

Some batsmen simply cannot stay still in their set-up; they feel they need to move prior to the bowler bowling. A trigger movement is that extra movement those batsmen make to get themselves into position as the bowler comes in to bowl. These should be explored in winter with the benefit of nets and throw downs.

How to do it

- Batsmen whose heads tend to fall off-side of their feet may try wiggling their toes. This allows them to focus on watching the ball and staying balanced.
- Others who fall over their front foot may incorporate a front foot press to stop themselves planting their front foot.
- Other triggers include the batsman moving their left and right feet back and across or simply lifting the left and right foot on the spot.
- Triggers can be mental as well as physical, for example saying 'watch the ball' as the bowler approaches.
- A batsman may experiment with different movements, but should remember triggers should feel natural.

Whichever trigger is adopted, it is crucial that you have completed your movement and are still when the bowler releases the ball.

Practice drill

- The coach simulates a bowling action when they deliver the ball, to allow the batsman to work out at what point they should implement their trigger. Too early, and the motion is pointless; too late and the batsman will be playing the shot off-balance and on the move.
- Move into a net environment and hone the timings against bowlers.

Problem and fix

- *The batsman's trigger is suddenly leaving them unbalanced.* The batsman may have grown, or simply started over-accentuating the trigger movement over time. Try going back to an orthodox stance.

For young batsmen who are still growing, triggers can often be misleading and disorientating as they increase the potential for movement in the stance, affecting the weight distribution of the batsman. That said, each batsman is different, and there are plenty of examples of top quality batsmen with pronounced triggers. The difference is, they are experienced players who are making their trigger decisions based on an in-depth understanding of their technique.

Footwork doesn't mean moving your feet all over the place. It's positioning.
Wilfred Rhodes, Yorkshire and England spinner, 1954

Back-lift

What it is

After the initial pick-up of the bat, whether it is a front or back-foot stroke, the back-lift should take place as the batsman moves to play the ball.

The point of the back-lift is to increase power into the shot with a free-flowing bat face. Without a back-lift the batsman would be limited to prodding at the ball.

How to do it

- The batsman's stance should be with the hands by the back pocket, lifting the bat back as far as is comfortable depending on what type of shot they intend to play.
- The batsman should practise moving forwards and backwards as their feet land in position, then rehearse and check the back-swing has occurred.
- Keep repeating until it becomes a natural process.

EXPERT COACHING TIP

The key thing to remember is that the back-lift should ideally be straight. There are examples of successful batsmen who haven't had straight back-lifts (notably Sir Donald Bradman) but for most players it makes sense to simplify things.

Problems and fixes

- *Not taking the bat back straight.* Use the drills opposite to work hard on making a straight back-lift routine.

Practice drill

- Get the batsman batting as usual in the nets. Place batting tees (or equivalent) on top of off and leg-stump to make sure that the back-swing goes straight back. If it doesn't, it will knock the poles over.
- The batsman should stand in front of a mirror, front on, and go through the range of movements of the shots, checking that they are taking the bat back straight.

Practice drills for the set-up

- The batsman should close their eyes and practise the pre-delivery routine (including tapping the bat on the ground). They should pick the bat up, open their eyes and check their pick-up and head position in the stance.
- The batsman should close their eyes again, and imagine they are to play a forward defence (see page 31) and let their head fall towards the ball. When the batsman feels they are about to fall, they should let their body follow. They should land with their front knee bent, head over the ball and a strong solid base to play off.
- The batsman should get someone to throw them tennis ball bobble-feeds or drop-feeds, and try to hit the ball on the half-volley on the second bounce. They should pick up the bat with both hands but drive with the top hand only. Alternatively, the batsman could get someone to roll the ball along the ground and try to hit it straight back along the line it came.

Problems and fixes for the set-up

- *Not picking the bat up straight.* Make sure that the hands are not pushing away from the body on back-lift causing the bat to move towards gully.

- *Stance gets too closed off.* Left shoulder gets too far around causing the bat to go behind leg-stump.

- *Bottom hand too tight and dominant.* This will cause closing of the bat face early and a loss of the left elbow through the shot. Keep the grip relaxed and evenly distributed.

- *Overbalancing.* Don't be too eager to get to the ball, otherwise the head moves early and there can be overbalancing.

Things to remember

The pick-up. Some players will use a very low pick-up of the bat when facing extreme pace.

The crease. Some batsmen like to stand a yard out of their crease (when the wicket-keeper is standing back) to disrupt the bowler's line and length, or to put a yard of pace on the ball if the wicket is slow and the bowler isn't quick enough. Equally some batsmen will stand deep in their crease to give them more time against pace bowling.

EQUIPMENT
Choosing a bat

Picking a bat that is the right size is vital for any cricketer, and particularly young cricketers. Nothing can hamper stroke-play like a bat that is too heavy or too big, while if a bat is too small it can affect the stance. While heavier bats can hit the ball harder, a batsman is just as likely to hit it hard with a lighter bat if it suits their timing of the ball.

To select the correct size, all players should follow some simple rules.

- Stand with the feet about shoulder-width apart, have the knees slightly bent and place the bat behind the right foot. The handle should rest against the left thigh about the height of the groin.
- The batsman should pick the bat up using the top hand only and see how long they can comfortably keep the bat in the pick-up position. If they struggle straight away, it is too heavy. They should try a few imaginary shots to get the feel and balance of the bat. Look at the grains on the bat face; these are lines that run down the bat. They should be equal distance apart.

EXPERT COACHING TIP

Think light. The heavier the bat, the more difficult it is to play certain shots and to control the bat, so you won't time the ball as you would like.

Batmaker's Expert Tips – from Salix Bats

Bats tend to be in traditional sizes, starting from size 3, 4, 5 and 6 up to Harrow and then on to short-handle and long-handle. There are starter sizes of 1 and 2 from certain manufacturers, while half-sizes may also be available direct from some manufacturers. The jump between each size is roughly an inch, so as a batsman moves up between the bats they'll find a size up is normally half-an-inch longer in the handle and half an inch longer in the blade.

In senior cricket, 95% of bats made are short-handles, and might be used by batsmen of heights ranging from 5ft 7ins to 6ft 5ins. Long handles put people off because they feel they lose control of the blade. Willow is a natural-growing tender, so weight varies from one bat to the next. A list of suggested weights and sizes is below.

The other interesting thing to look out for when buying a bat is the style and grade of woods on offer. In recent years big, light bats have been in fashion. Traditionally the best willow (Grade 1) is made from sap wood (the lower part of the tree where there is moisture in the wood). This makes for stronger, more durable willow, but because of the extra moisture the bats tend to be a little heavier.

To accommodate the trend for bigger bats, bat-makers have started using willow from higher up the tree (Grade 2). This allows them to make big bats with bigger hitting areas at lighter weights, but because the willow is drier there are more breakages. A batsman might find they get better value from a bat with a slightly smaller back.

Size of bat	suggested weight of bat	suggested height of batsman
Short-handle	2'7–2'9	5'7"+
Harrow	2'4–2'6	5'4"–5'7"
Size 6	2'2–2'4	5'2"–5'4"
Size 5	2'1–2'2	4'11"–5'2"
Size 4	1'13–1'15	4'9"–4'11"
Size 3	1'1–1'12	4'6"–4'9"

Anything below this should use size 1 or 2.

Other equipment

Helmet. All young players up to the age of 18 (16 in Australia) must now wear helmets, and a young batsman should never be allowed to take guard not wearing one. The England and Wales Cricket Board (ECB) safety guidance is as follows.

- Helmets with a faceguard or grille should be worn when batting against a hard cricket ball in matches and in practice sessions.
- Young players should regard a helmet with a faceguard as a normal item of protective equipment when batting, together with pads, gloves and, for boys, an abdominal protector.

Batting gloves. Should be comfortable and provide adequate protection and padding in the instance that a ball hits the batsman's hand.

Padding. Pads protect the batsman's legs from the ball. The young batsman should choose pads that allow them to run properly between the wickets. Thigh pads and inner-thigh pads can also be used to give added protection and confidence. Boys should wear an abdominal protector at all times.

Batting terms explained

Strike rate: The number of runs the batsman scores per hundred balls. This is something the batsman would be looking to increase in one-day cricket and Twenty20.

Average: The average number of runs a batsman scores each innings. An average of 40 is normally the sign of a good batsman, and over 50 an excellent one.

RUNNING BETWEEN THE WICKETS

Watch a Twenty20 game and you may not believe it, but cricket is not all about boundaries. The majority of scoring shots are singles and twos, but to make them count, a batsman needs to know how to run between the wickets.

Running between the wickets can be a very hard skill for inexperienced batsmen to master. It involves very good judgement skills – both of how far the ball has travelled, and how long the fielding side will take to return the ball.

The calling batsman should also think about their partner at the other end, and whether they will be able to make their ground safely too. Good running between the wickets can put the fielding side under pressure and ultimately be the difference between winning and losing a match, especially in limited-over cricket.

Calling

What it is

When a batsman is running between the wickets they need to communicate clearly so the other batsman knows whether they are expected to run or not.

How to do it

- The batsman must call loudly and decisively when running between the wicket. 'Yes', 'No' or 'Wait' (followed by yes or no).

- Calls are made by the striking batsman when the ball has gone in front of square, and by the non-striker when it has gone behind square. This is because the non-striker can see the whole picture, and will be running to the danger end.

- If the batsman feels their partner has called for a run when there isn't one, they should call 'No' loudly and clearly. There may still be time for them to get safely back in their crease. A batsman should never feel pressured into running if they don't think a run is possible.

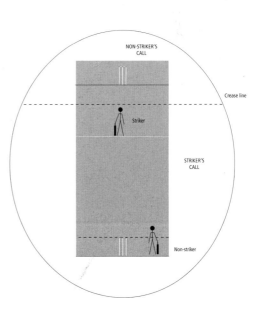

NON-STRIKER'S CALL

Crease line

Striker

STRIKER'S CALL

Non-striker

Running

What it is

Running the first run hard can put pressure on the fielding team, induce mistakes and give the batsmen the best chance of turning one run into two.

How to do it

- Hold the bat across the body and pump the arms and legs hard when setting off. The head should be kept down in this stage.

- Halfway through the run the batsman should lift their head to look for where the ball is. The batsman's stride will lengthen, and they can decide whether or not to turn for a second run.

- When going for a single be sure to ground the bat when entering the crease. A part of the bat or the body should be over the crease line before the fielding side break the bails or the batsman will be run out.

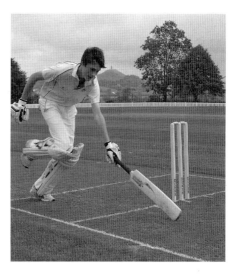

Turning for two
What it is
Once the batsman knows there is a chance of two runs, it's vital that they turn quickly in the crease to get back for a second.

How to do it
- When turning for another run the batsman should get low again and place the bat in the correct hand so that when they turn at the crease they are facing the right way to see the fielder.

- As the batsman approaches the crease they should sink the hips and lean back slightly, running the bat into the crease, but not the rest of the body.

- Push off hard with the leg closest to the crease, into the technique for starting a run described above.

- Failure to ground the bat at the end of the first run when running two will see the umpire signal for 'one short'. Make sure to ground the bat in the crease at the end of each run.

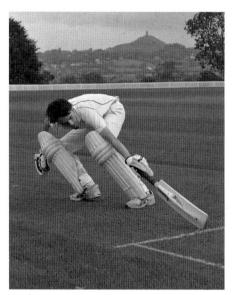

This is an example of one short

Back up at the bowler's end and anticipate the chance of a run off every ball.

When running a quick single make sure you slide the bat a metre out from the crease. This will give you the best chance of getting in quickly.

Run the first hard to put pressure on the fielding side, they might fumble the ball and give you a chance of another run. Fielding sides hate being put under pressure at any level.

Practice drills
- Gather a group of batsmen at one end of the wicket. As they start running the coach shouts either off-side or leg-side and how many. A batsman is out if they turn incorrectly or their bat is in the wrong hand as they turn for two.
- Assemble two teams of batsmen and fielders. The coach stands behind the stumps at the wicket-keeper's end, the fielders at extra-cover, and one batsman at each end. The coach rolls the ball out into the off-side and shouts 'go'. The batsmen are trying to take a quick single, while the fielders are trying to run them out, at either end depending on the angle of the ball.

LINE AND LENGTH

Before the batsman plays any shots it's important to learn a little about line and length. What line and length the ball is delivered at determines what shot the batsman will play.

Line refers to the direction the ball is coming to in relation to the leg-stump. For example, if a ball pitches in line with off-stump it would be said to have an off-stump line. A ball down the leg-side would be one that pitches outside of leg-stump and keeps going straight on.

Length is the spot on the wicket that the ball pitches. Different lengths are described on the following pages.

LINE LENGTH AND SHOT SELECTION

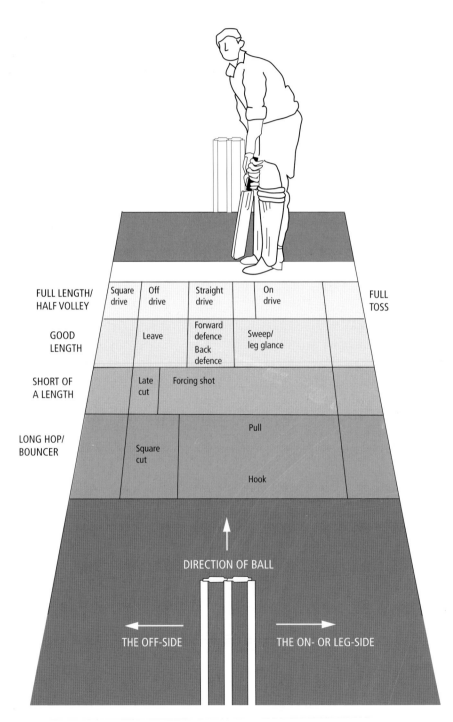

FULL LENGTH/ HALF VOLLEY	Square drive	Off drive	Straight drive	On drive			**FULL TOSS**
GOOD LENGTH		Leave	Forward defence / Back defence	Sweep/ leg glance			
SHORT OF A LENGTH		Late cut	Forcing shot				
LONG HOP/ BOUNCER		Square cut		Pull			
				Hook			

DIRECTION OF BALL

THE OFF-SIDE   THE ON- OR LEG-SIDE

TERMS (see opposite page)

Long hop

What it is: The long hop is the ball batsmen love and bowlers dread. It's a short ball lacking the pace to trouble the batsman, and is a great opportunity for a boundary.

Where does it pitch? Closer to the bowler's feet than the batsman's.

Bouncer

What it is: The quick bowler's long hop, but because of the extra pace it is an excellent aggressive weapon for the fast bowler. A good bouncer might target the armpit up to the head, but a bad one might also give the batsman the opportunity to hook or cut.

Where does it pitch? Halfway down the wicket, or just inside the bowler's half depending on the surface.

Short of a length

What it is: Confusingly this can be either a good ball or a poor ball depending on the surface. If it's wide the batsman can thump it, but if it's straight it can be an effective delivery on a good pitch, pushing the batsman back on his crease.

Where does it pitch? Fuller than a bouncer, shorter than a good length.

Good length

What it is: A good length is that length which leaves the batsman uncertain of whether to play forward or back. Normally this is about four metres from the batsman.

Where does it pitch? On the length where the batsman is unsure whether to play back or forward.

Half-volley

What it is: The half-volley lands in the perfect slot for the batsman to hit the ball just as it bounces, so negating any seam or swing the bowler has put on it.

Where does it pitch: On the perfect length for the batsman to reach it as it bounces.

Yorker

What it is: Called the 'toe crusher' because it pitches on the batsman's toes, it is a very effective delivery when bowled with pace and swing as it can be very difficult to dig out.

Where does it pitch: On the batsman's toes.

Full toss

What it is: A full toss is essentially a free-hit for the batsman.

Where does it pitch: It doesn't.

Beamer

What it is: One step worse than the full toss, a beamer is a ball that reaches the batsman on the full above waist height for a quick bowler, or above shoulder height for a slow bowler. One to get out of the way of.

Where does it pitch: On the batsman.

Iain O'Brien on batsmen through a bowler's eyes
What mistakes do you see batsmen making most often?

They didn't wait long enough. The bowler's always going to bowl a bad ball, no matter what. I used to get wickets by almost boring batsmen out, rather than by getting them out. Against that type of bowling, if the batter does wait, I'll have to change my tactics, and the batter will get balls to score off. A lot of batters didn't wait long enough, and tried to score boundaries off deliveries they should have been defending.

How difficult is it to bowl at someone who takes the game to you?

When guys like Virender Sehwag and Tillekeratne Dilshan came out and were ultra-aggressive to good deliveries, that was one of the hardest things to deal with and to overcome. Where do you go to as a bowler in that situation? Do you change what you were doing or do you hang tough to your plan and try and dismiss them that way? It can be a no-win situation.

How does a batsman get on top of a bowler?

If the bowler has to change his game-plan then the batter has won. As a bowling unit you tend to have a Plan A, Plan B or a Plan C for an international batter. If you're getting down to Plan C then the batter is having a pretty good day.

What body language does a bowler pick up on?
The best batters acknowledge good deliveries, and accept that occasionally there are going to be deliveries that they can't get near. They keep themselves quite flat-line, they don't get too up or too down. Then you see the guys who are fighting with themselves and that can be quite good fun, because you can have a good little battle with them. If they are fighting with themselves it is easier to stay on top of the batter, especially with some noise from the fielders.

Iain O'Brien is a medium-pacer who played 22 Tests for New Zealand between 2005 and 2009

SHOTS

2.

Look at Border. He's scored 10,000 Test runs and he's only got three shots – the cut, the cover drive and the pull.
JACK BIRKENSHAW, LEICESTERSHIRE MANAGER, ADMIRING THE APPROACH OF ALLAN BORDER, 1994

So that's the set-up, now onto the harder stuff – the shots.

If a batsman can master all the shots in this book, then theoretically they should be able to play all around the wicket and have an answer for every type of ball. It's that simple.

Yet even the best players will struggle with some shots. Of all the shots in this book it may be that a particular batsman will never touch some of them, regard others with suspicion, and only trust a few to be their main run-getters. That is normal, some players develop techniques that suit some shots, and not others. International careers have been built on a few shots played well. What is important is the ability of a batsman to self-analyse, in other words to be aware of where their strengths and weaknesses are, and then be disciplined enough to let that help them in the middle.

If a batsman keeps edging cover drives, it may be that it's best not to keep playing them until they've worked on them in the nets. It may be that a batsman is good on their legs, so leaving the ball well outside off-stump will make bowlers bowl straighter and give them more balls on their pads.

Practice is the single most important thing when it comes to learning a new shot. A batsman should get used to the idea of working on a new skill over and over again, alone or as part of a small net session, until they are happy with it. Experimenting with something in the middle is rarely a good idea, more often that not it will cost the batsman his wicket.

Finally, just a few things to remember

1. Unless it's specified otherwise, it is assumed that a right-handed batsman is facing a right-arm over the wicket bowler.
2. It's good to watch the great players, study their techniques, and learn from them. Throughout this book references have been made to current or past

players. Look them up, there should be video footage of them all on the internet or other resources that allow you to appreciate their abilities for yourself.

3. While it's important to have role models and study the great players (as above), it's vital that each batsman retains their individuality. A batsman should concentrate on building their own technique and finding what works for them, rather than what works for other people.

4. If things go wrong in the middle, don't panic. Go back to basics and re-examine the set-up. More often than not there's a simple explanation and an easy fix.

Most of all, enjoy it.

Being left-handed

The left-hander should mirror all the technical information that has been given to the right-handed batsman.

Many left-handers prefer a slightly open stance (see page 9) as the majority of bowlers come from right-arm over the wicket and tend to bowl a lot at their pads.

A left-hander might align their shoulders with first or second slip and draw the front foot back slightly from the line of the off-stump. This will improve leg-side play but can make it harder to get the front foot across to the off-side.

When facing a right-arm round the wicket or left-arm over bowler then the left-hander should revert to a more orthodox side-on stance (see page 6).

The left-hander should make an extra effort to make sure they are comfortable with where their off-stump is, as they will be facing a large amount of deliveries that are coming across them.

EXPERT COACHING TIP When making any changes to their set-up the batsman should be aware of exactly what the implications will be for their technique.

FRONT-FOOT SHOTS

Any fool can play forward.
A.C. MacLaren, England captain, 1921

Forward defence

What it is

If a batsman only learns one shot from this book it should be this one – behind every good batsman is a good forward defensive shot. Without it, the batsman won't survive long enough to score any runs, because this is the shot that stops a straight ball from hitting the stumps.

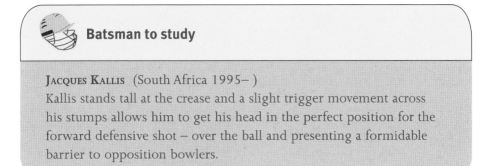

Batsman to study

Jacques Kallis (South Africa 1995–)
Kallis stands tall at the crease and a slight trigger movement across his stumps allows him to get his head in the perfect position for the forward defensive shot – over the ball and presenting a formidable barrier to opposition bowlers.

When to play it

Play to a straight, good length delivery.

How to play it

*   Head and shoulder lead with left shoulder dipping into shot. Keep a comfortable front leg astride to the ball. Keep the front knee bent and feel the back foot coming off of the ground.

- The bat speed decelerates and the hands are softened on the handle with a high front elbow. This allows the ball to hit the bat and drop down with the angle of the bat face pointing towards the ground.

- Eyes are level and watching the ball on to the bat.

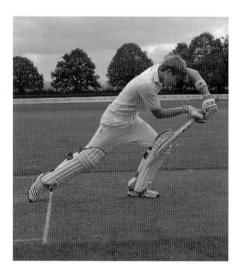

Problems and fixes

- *Hands too hard on the handle.* This will cause stabbing at the ball. Relax the grip, and the defensive stroke.

- *Back foot spins around.* This causes an unstable base and overbalancing, while forcing the batsman's left shoulder open. Try and keep the weight evenly balanced between the feet even when playing forward.

- *Head not over the ball.* This leads to playing the ball in the air and the possibility of being caught out. Keep the head over the ball.

- *Pushing the bottom hand beyond the top hand.* The bat face will now be facing upright causing the ball to go in the air. The top hand should stay in front of the bottom hand at all times.

Practice drill

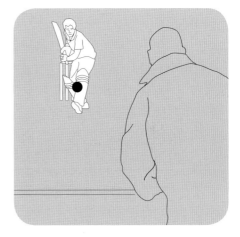

- The coach throws tennis balls from behind a line drawn six metres from the batsman. The batsman has to play forward defence with soft hands. The ball must not cross the line otherwise the batsman is out.
- To intensify the degree of difficulty introduce close fielders, make the ball bounce higher and make it spin more.

Batting with soft hands

This technique is applied to all defensive shots. The bottom hand of the grip is virtually released from the bat handle allowing the ball to hit the bat and drop down in front of the batsman as opposed to going hard at the ball.

This technique might be used on a turning wicket with close-in catchers or to a fast rising delivery. Soft hands will help absorb the pace and hopefully the ball will drop short of the close in catchers. This also allows the batsman to 'drop' the ball and run, thus rotating the strike.

Practice drill

- The coach throws tennis balls with close in catchers. The batsman has no front pad and is not allowed to be aggressive. The bat should be played slightly in front of the pad. Move on to cricket balls or bowling machine.

THE LEAVE
Why it is important

A 'good leave' is often followed by praise from the coach. It can be as good as playing a scoring shot and shows the batsman is aware of where his off-stump is. Leaving the ball well, early in his innings, allows the batsman a number of 'sighters', time to gauge the pace and amount of movement in the pitch, and the chance to assess what type of bowler they are facing.

Leaving the ball outside off-stump will often result in the bowler bowling straighter. This enables the batsman to play closer to his body – a safer and more productive option than chasing at wide deliveries.

The leave is a particularly important skill for **left-handed batsmen** who face a lot of deliveries from right-arm over bowlers slanting the ball across them. Leaving the ball well means the bowler is forced to bowl at the body, leading to increased scoring opportunities off the batsman's legs.

The key things to think about when leaving a delivery are **line** and **length**.

- On hard pitches of consistent bounce the batsman can get away with leaving a straight delivery on **length** alone when it pitches short of a good length, but they should be wary of attempting this on pitches of variable or low bounce where there is a risk of the ball keeping low and hitting the stumps.

- Always take into account what the bowler is doing with the ball when deciding to leave a ball on **line**. If they've nibbled a couple back towards the stumps then leaving one just outside the off-stump might not be a good idea. This is the area known as the 'corridor of uncertainty', and how a batsman comes to judge balls in this area will play a large part in their level of success.

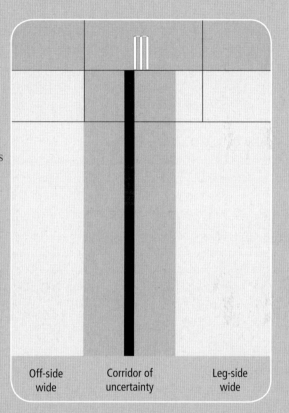

Off-side wide   Corridor of uncertainty   Leg-side wide

Practice drill

Similar to the practice drill that accompanied taking guard, the batsman should get a coach to throw balls on or around off-stump and practise playing at only those deliveries that they think are going to hit the stumps.

DRIVES

Drives are temptation. They look great when the batsman catches them perfectly, but pick the wrong time to play them and it can be an easy way to lose a wicket. The drive is played to full-length deliveries, and that gilt-edged chance to score runs can cause the batsman to play loosely and lose control of the shot. The key is to stay on top of the ball, and not give catching opportunities by edging behind the wicket or hitting in the air in front of it.

Key to executing the shot is choosing balls that are the right line and length to be driven – usually those that are over-pitched – full-tosses or half-volley length. It's also important for a batsman to think about what type of pitch it is before they start playing drives. Is it a slow pitch? If so, the drive becomes a high-risk shot, and the batsman needs to make sure they wait for the ball as long as possible before going through with the stroke. If the batsman is too aggressive and plays the shot too early there is the chance of an easy catch for the fielding side. If it's a good pitch it's worth checking exactly where the fielders are to give the best chance of missing them.

Different types of drive take their names from the area of the field that they are hit towards. A straight drive is played to a straight delivery and goes back between the bowler and mid-off. A cover-drive is played to a wider delivery and hit squarer, through the cover fielders, while an on-drive is played to a ball closer to a batsman's legs and hit back through mid-on.

> **It's hard work making batting look effortless.**
> DAVID GOWER, ENGLAND BATSMAN, 1989

Straight drive

What it is

Theoretically the most logical shot in cricket, the batsman eases the ball back where it came from, past the bowler. If only it were as easy as that.

When to play it

This is played to an over-pitched delivery, either a full toss or half-volley, on a straight-ish line.

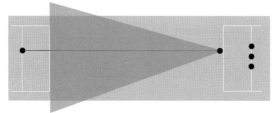

How to play it

- Simplified, this is merely an extension of the forward defence. The head and left shoulder dip and, when moving into the shot, take the hands back further than for the defensive shot. Making sure the eyes are watching the ball, the front foot lands next to the ball with bent front knee.

- Accelerate the hands through the shot, keeping the front elbow (steering wheel) high and through the line of the stroke.

- Either extend the hands out to finish in a checked drive position (see box on next page) or break the wrists and allow full flourish and finish with bat over the shoulder.

Vɪʀᴇɴᴅᴇʀ Sᴇʜᴡᴀɢ (India 2001–)
Sehwag's driving is not as technically perfect as Tendulkar's, but is a good example of the more aggressive, modern approach to batting. While he is always looking to get at the bowler, he also looks to hit straight, presenting a full face of the bat whenever possible.

Checked drive

The checked drive is a controlled stroke where the batsman pushes their hands through the ball, but stops the motion at the point where the wrists would break.

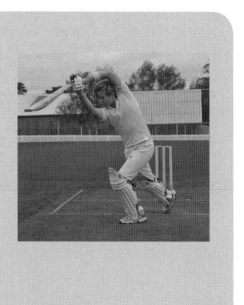

A batsman might use the checked drive when they are being cautious, perhaps while opening the batting, or on a good pitch with a quick outfield where good timing is enough for the ball to beat the infield and reach the boundary.

On-drive

What it is

One of the hardest shots to play as balance is crucial. The on-drive is a shot that is the hallmark of a great player. This shot is at risk with increasing innovation, as younger, wristier players look to whip balls through mid-wicket that their predecessors would have leant on down the ground.

Sachin Tendulkar drives through mid-on against England in 2011.

When to play it

This is played to an over-pitched delivery (a full toss or half volley) on a middle-and-leg line.

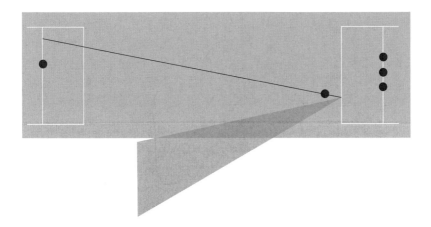

How to play it

- Head and shoulder lead. Take a smaller stride than the straight or cover drive – open the left shoulder and the front foot points straighter down the ground.

- The batsman should wait for the ball as long as possible and impact under the eyes. Keep the left knee bent, with the back foot heel off the ground.

- Push the hands through the ball, with the left elbow staying on the line of shot. Don't try and hit it too hard. Aiming to hit the ball for two and timing it well will often see it go for four.

Sᴀᴄʜɪɴ Tᴇɴᴅᴜʟᴋᴀʀ (India 1989–)
So perfect is Tendulkar's balance at the crease that he is worth
studying for virtually every shot in this book. If his straight drive is
his signature shot, the on-drive is where his technique is illustrated
best – a perfectly still head position and transfer of weight leaving
him in total control of one of the most difficult shots in the game.

Cover or square drive

What it is

The most common of the beautiful shots, this is also the drive that the young
batsman will find easiest to play. Put the front foot to the ball, lean on it, and
watch it travel to the boundary. The square drive goes through point off the front
foot, and the cover drive through cover.

When to play it

Played to a half-volley or full toss pitching wide of the off-stump.

How to play it

- Head and shoulder lead with shoulder dipping. As the batsman is looking to hit squarer, the left shoulder should turn more to the line of the ball with part of the back facing the bowler.

- The front knee bends and lands next to the line of the ball. Keep the head still and the eyes level. Watch the ball onto the bat.

- Impact the ball under the eyes, keeping a high left elbow through the shot and the hands working as one.

The cover drive is the most beautiful stroke in batsmanship.
Does that throw any light on why I am a self-admitted lover of all
things British and traditional?
COLIN COWDREY, IN HIS AUTOBIOGRAPHY, MCC, IN 1976

Batsman to study

IAN BELL (England 2004–)
Bell had been earmarked as a potential star from his early teens due to
the type of classical technique rarely seen in modern batsmen. Watch
the position of his head, his balanced weight distribution and how
his hands flow through the ball as he strokes, not smashes, the ball to
the cover boundary.

Practice drills for driving
- Tennis ball bobble- and drop-feeds. The batsman should pick up the bat with two hands but drive with only the top hand.
- Introduce targets for cover drive/straight drive/on-drive.
- Coach calls the type of shot prior to releasing the ball for the batsman to play.
- To intensify, use a bowling machine with the ball swinging out and in from the batsman.
- Another trick is to use different weighted balls during drop-feeds or bobble-feeds (building up to throw-downs) to the batsman. This makes the batsman really watch the ball onto the bat, and react according to the bounce of the delivery.

Problems and fixes
- *Ball goes in the air when driving.* The batsman may be leaning back.

- *Straight drives go through leg side.* Check the grip and that the left elbow is acting as the steering wheel for the shot. The bottom hand might be too dominant and closing the bat face. Check the head is not to the off-side of the ball on impact, as the batsman won't be able to hit through the off-side.

- *Can't seem to time the ball.* Is the batsman just pushing at it? – Lack of momentum may be caused by a low back swing in set-up when moving into the shot.

- *Batsman edges drive behind.* Was the ball too wide to play?

- *Keep squaring up.* Check that the batsman's back foot is not swivelling.

BACK-FOOT SHOTS

So far so good, but things get a little tougher now with the batsman getting their chance to show their courage during the back-foot shots.

The higher the level the batsman is playing at and the quicker the bowling they are facing, the more likely they are to be playing shots on the back foot. Back-foot shots are played when the ball is bowled shorter and bounces higher, forcing the batsman to get on their back foot to be in control of the shot.

Be wary of the height of the ball when playing on the back foot. When playing defensively, anything that is passing over the stumps and not straight at the body can be left alone. When attacking, any ball that is bouncing over head height will be very difficult to control, as will any cross-batted shots on a pitch that is offering variable bounce. The good news with back-foot shots is that there can be more time and opportunity to free the arms and play attacking shots.

As a batsman moves from U-13 to senior cricket there comes a point when the bowling becomes quicker and the player must seek to develop his back-foot play. This is best done over the winter, with time taken to build confidence and take away the fear factor ahead of what can be testing first experiences against the short ball.

As the player gets more experienced, it's vital that they do not allow the fear factor to get the better of them. The quicker the ball comes, the quicker it can go, and there's nothing that helps build a total like wayward short-pitched bowling.

They were nearly all made off the back foot.
JACK HOBBS, EXPLAINING WHY THE 85 FIRST-CLASS CENTURIES MADE AFTER THE FIRST WORLD WAR DID NOT MATCH THOSE OF HIS YOUTH

Back-foot defence

What it is

If the forward defensive is the batsman's right leg, the back defensive is his left leg. This may not be an attacking shot, but it makes a statement to the bowler that the batsman is brave and will get right in behind the ball. This shot defends the body, so without it the batsman won't get anywhere.

 Batsman to study

MICHAEL ATHERTON (England 1988–2000)
As an opening batsman at a time when every side in world cricket had a formidable opening bowling partnership, Atherton spent a lot of time defending on the back foot. Key was getting back and across, and keeping his eyes in position so he was right over the ball when defending. This technique served him well in his career-defining innings – a 10 hour 45 minute 185* to save a Test for England in Johannesburg in 1995.

When to play it

Played to a delivery shorter than a good length, the height is on or above stump height.

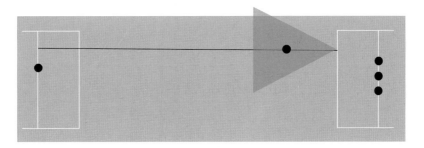

How to play it

- The ball is straight so there is no attacking option. Head and shoulder lead to the line of the ball. As the batsman steps back, the back swing occurs and the left shoulder gets into the line of the delivery.

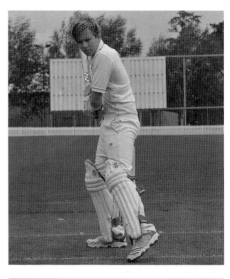

- The back foot should be side on. The left foot is drawn back but merely acts as a balance. The head should be in front of the back foot on the line of the ball. Keep a high left elbow with a relaxed bottom-hand grip.

- Hit the ball under the eyes with the bat face angling down.

Problems and fixes

- *Popping the ball in the air.* The weight may be too far on the back foot, meaning the hands will be pushed at the ball and the ball will go in the air. Even when on the back foot the batsman's weight should be forward, and they should allow the ball to hit the bat when defending with soft hands.

- *Batsman getting squared up.* Rather than landing square the back foot lands pointing towards extra cover, as the bat path comes down from third slip or gully. An edge is almost inevitable.

- *Gripping the bat too tightly.* This can be out of fear, and cause a stabbing at the ball. Relax the grip, and the mind.

- *Backing away to leg.* When facing quicker bowling, batsmen often turn away from the ball and run away to leg: don't. The batsman should have courage and get in line, as the ball is far less likely to hit them if they can see where it is going and evade it. The batsman should trust that the work they have put in against the short ball will be enough to see them through.

Practice drill

- Mirror work. Move back and across playing an imaginary delivery with the eyes closed. The batsman should then open their eyes and check their position.
- Starting with tennis balls, try throw downs bounced straight at the body. Build up to cricket balls and then ultimately the bowling machine.

Back-foot drive

What it is

An extension of the back-foot defensive, it sounds simple but it's a difficult shot to master.

Batsman to study

VIRENDER SEHWAG (1999–)
Sehwag is one of the most destructive attacking batsmen the game has seen, which explains why he is an example for more than one shot. He looks to attack every ball – key to that is a quick eye for judging line and length and a stance that allows him to get forward and back quickly. There is nothing over-complicated about his back-foot drive. He gets in a good position early, and extends his hands and arms through the ball to send it flying to the fence.

When to play it

This shot is played to a back of the length delivery offering width outside the off-stump, but not enough to square cut.

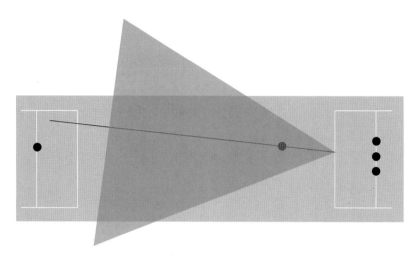

How to play it

- Head and shoulder should lead with the left shoulder turning into the line of the ball.

- Back foot lands parallel to the crease while the front foot follows but only for balance purposes.

- The head position is three to four inches forward of the back foot.

- Keeping a high front elbow, hit the ball under the eyes with a cradling motion with both arms going through the line of the ball.

General problems and fixes for back-foot play

- *Going straight back with right foot instead of back and across.* This causes the bat to be a long way from the body meaning a loss of power and control of the bat face. The ball tends to go towards backward point or slip.
- *No power in the shot.* This happens because the batsman hasn't got their weight distribution right – the head has gone over the back foot so there is no solid base established.
- *The bat face comes across the line of the ball.* The bottom hand is too dominant, which causes the left elbow to lose its line of the shot early. The batsman is then unable to direct the left elbow and hands through the line of the shot successfully.

Practice drill

- The batsman stands with right leg bent and off the ground.

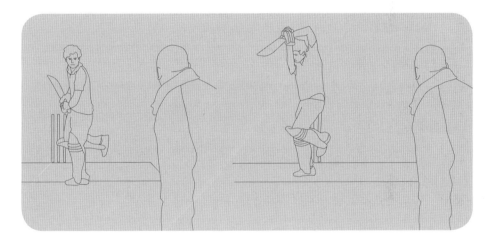

- The coach from a distance of four metres, underarms a full toss outside the off-stump just above stump height.
- The batsman has to lead quickly with their head and shoulder across to the line of the ball.
- The batsman now has to transfer to their right leg with the left leg bent and off the ground. The weight should be forward of the back foot when hitting the ball then allow the left leg to step forward after the shot. Once mastered, the coach can introduce 'throw downs' and the bowling machine to help groove the shot.

> *At the crease my attitude to three bouncers an over has been that, if I'm playing well enough, three bouncers an over should be worth 12 runs to me.*
>
> IAN CHAPPELL, AUSTRALIA BATSMAN, OPPOSING LIMITATIONS ON BOUNCERS, 1970S

The hook

What it is

The hook shot is played to a quick delivery of throat height and above so when a batsman chooses to play it, they are accepting the element of risk involved and telling the bowler that they will not be intimidated.

It is not wise for a batsman to play a hook shot unless they are confident in the conditions (for example the pace of the pitch) and aware of the field, as it is a shot that will go in the air and therefore be easily caught.

Hook shots go mostly behind square.

A good base position for the hook shot is essential, enabling the batsman to pull out of the shot at the last minute if they feel they are losing control of the stroke.

Viv Richards (West Indies 1974–91)
Few before or since can have played the hook as destructively as Viv Richards. Richards, captain of the West Indies during their era of startling dominance, made a difficult shot look as natural as swatting flies, combining natural timing with brutal power.

Viv Richards hooks Ian Botham with ease.

When to play it

The hook is played to a short delivery known as a 'bouncer'.

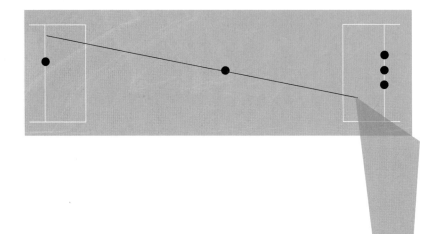

How to play it

- The height of the delivery should be usually chest and upwards, ideally over the left shoulder. Quick feet are essential for the hook. The right foot should go back and across with the toes pointing down the wicket.

- The head and eyes should be still, with the weight forward. The left leg is drawn back but only acts as a balance. Take the hands back to a high position.

- Contact is made with fully extended arms in front of the eyes. As the batsman hits the ball, the chest rotates and the body follows, finishing with a pivot of the feet.

Problems and fixes

- *Hooking deliveries above head height or from outside off-stump.* The batsman will discover in the practice drills that they lose control with these shots, resulting in a top edge and maybe a catch given.

- *Head position back.* Again power and control lost.

- *Trying to hit the ball too hard.* This causes a top edge.

Practice drill

- Under-arm feeds with a tennis ball from close range.
- Different height feeds to allow the batsman to explore which height and line he is comfortable with.
- The coach moves back and engages in 'bounced throw downs' and then on to the bowling machine.
- Try to hit fours and sixes from similar feeds on the bowling machine.

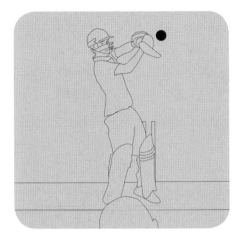

Allan Lamb on hooking and facing fast bowling

Allan Lamb was a South-African-born batsman who played for England in the 1980s and early 90s. Lamb was brought up on hard South African pitches and the true bounce made him an excellent player of the short ball. He needed to be – West Indies were the dominant side of the era, their four quick bowlers terrifying batsmen the world over.

'Holding, Marshall and co. wanted to keep one guy down one end and just bomb him, and eventually they would get him. But if you looked to score runs, to hit the bad ball and look positive, not taking them on by hooking and such, then the game changed. Suddenly you didn't have four or five slips, short-leg, and a man on the hook.

'I believed, which perhaps some of the other guys didn't. Some would say, "How are we going to score a run against these guys?!" Be patient and be positive, that's how I saw it.

'Also I had a technique that worked. On quick wickets against quick bowling you don't get in behind the ball, because if it lifts a bit off a length how are you going to get out of the way? So you try to stay inside of the ball, or you got onto the other side. If you stayed inside the ball you could cut, and if the ball came the other side you could pull.

'The big thing was to keep still at the crease and watch the ball. I learnt early that you were never going to get hit if you watched the ball. I always had a thing when I played against the quick bowlers where I would watch the wrist. Sometimes you could see the seam, and the quicker the wrist came down the shorter the ball was going to be. That was vital. I didn't love playing against them but it was always a challenge.'

This interview originally appeared in the Wisden Cricketer

Allan Lamb, who played 79 Tests for England between 1982 and 1992.

Pull shot
What it is
Maybe the most natural shot in the game, and one that can give great confidence when played well. The pull shot is a more controlled version of the instinctive movement made when first picking up a cricket bat – the cross-batted swipe. It is also a lower risk shot than the hook – most batsmen will look to pull along the ground.

Key to playing the pull shot well is an ability to anticipate the length of the ball early and correctly, allowing the batsman to get on the back foot, free up their arms and hit the bowler through the leg side. Don't get too aggressive on the shot, watch the ball for as long as possible and roll the wrists at the last moment to keep the ball down.

It can be a useful shot to manipulate the field – whatever the batsman does with the pull they should have conviction and go through with the shot.

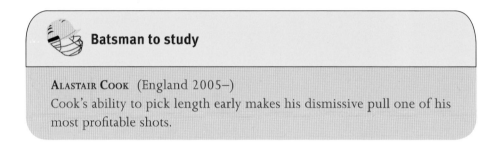

Batsman to study

ALASTAIR COOK (England 2005–)
Cook's ability to pick length early makes his dismissive pull one of his most profitable shots.

When to play it
This is an attacking cross-batted shot played to a long hop, bouncing up at waist height between a line of outside off-stump to just outside the leg-stump. It is bowled normally by a spin or medium-paced bowler.

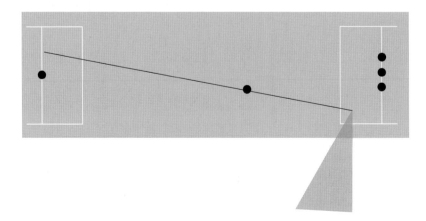

How to play it

- Quick feet are needed to get into position as early as possible. The head should lead to the line of the ball. Take the right leg back and across with the toe pointing down the wicket. Open the left leg up to the leg side allowing the batsman to face chest on back up the wicket.

- The head position should be forward towards the bowler. Adopt a high to low motion with the bat and the arms fully extended on impact of the ball.

- The batsman will need strong wrists to ensure the bat path stays constant. Watch the ball for as long as possible, then roll the wrists after impact of the ball. The head and eyes should remain still looking back up the wicket until after contact of the ball.

Problems and fixes

- *No power in the shot.* The batsman's arms may be tucked in and not fully extended – this means no power, usually resulting in a top edge and potential catch given.

- *The ball is going in the air.* The batsman's head position may be leaning back over their feet, resulting in loss of timing and the ball being hit uppishly.

- *Variable-bounce pitch.* This is where a delivery will either bounce up or down from the same spot, potentially resulting in a top edge catch or an under edge, dragging the ball on to the stumps.

EXPERT COACHING TIP

Assess the pitch, the field and the situation before you decide to play the pull shot. If you are going to take a risk, make sure it is a calculated one.

Practice drill

- Use a plastic stump as a ball tee – the batsman starts in a pull shot position and hits a series of balls.
- Begin in your normal stance and then move into the shot. Start with underarm feeds, then bounced feeds and finally bowling machine feeds, which should all be fed at waist height.
- Work very hard on getting the feet quickly into position.

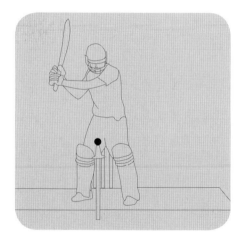

Ducking and evasion
What it is

If the batsman gets to a high enough level, the chances are they'll want to know how to duck and sway properly. We've talked already about the hook and the pull, but there is a third option. The batsman doesn't have to play at the ball if it gets too big on them, or if they don't think they can control the stroke. But if they want to leave the ball, they'll have to get their head out of the way first, while ensuring that the ball doesn't hit them.

 Batsman to study

MICHAEL ATHERTON (England 1989–2001)
Atherton's famous duel with South Africa's Allan Donald in 1998 is an excellent example of a batsman doing everything possible to evade a succession of head-hunters. Atherton was unlucky to play in an era during which nearly every side had a bowler capable of making the batsman duck and weave.

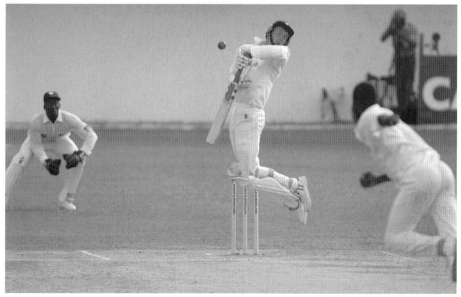

Michael Atherton evades a bouncer from Courtney Walsh of the West Indies.

When to play it

To a short ball, bouncing around head height, from a quick bowler that the batsman is looking to get out of the way of.

How to do it

- **Duck**: If the bounce is consistent, ducking is an option. If it's variable then it becomes very dangerous, as the ball might keep low and hit the batsman.

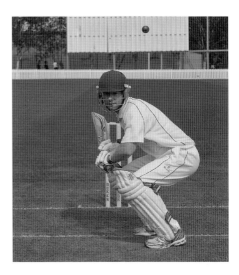

- **Evade**: Watch the ball closely, and move the head either side of it at the last possible moment. The batsman should be wary of which way the ball is swinging or seaming when deciding which side of the ball to go.

Practice drills

- See the drills in playing fast bowling, page 101. For more on hooking, pulling and facing fast bowling, see pages 99–101.

The square cut

The cut was never a business stroke.
WILFRED RHODES ON THE RISKS OF THE CUT SHOT

What it is

There is no shot in cricket as emphatic as the square cut. Even though it is played on the off-side, it is a cross-batted shot – the width of the delivery giving the batsman the opportunity to free his arms and thrash the ball square through the off-side.

The batsman typically gets the opportunity to square cut when a quick bowler errs in his line. The square cut relies on a natural swing of the arms so it is important to make sure that the ball is not too close or too far away when playing the shot.

Batsman to study

ROBIN SMITH (England 1988–96)
Smith square-cutting the West Indies quicks in his grille-less helmet was an iconic image of cricket in the early 1990s. Smith's square cut was dismissive and defiant at the same time, and it needed to be – Malcolm Marshall and co. didn't bowl many bad balls. Smith was raised on South African pitches, so was used to true bounce and the ball coming into the bat, and well drilled to the point of being instinctive in getting into position quickly to play the stroke.

When to play it

This shot is played to a short, wide delivery outside the off-stump.

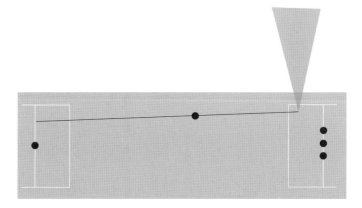

How to play it

- Lead with the head and shoulder, turning the left shoulder towards the line of point.

- Take a step back, landing with the right foot either parallel to the crease or slightly behind point. The back knee should be slightly bent. The front foot stays in its original position. All the batsman's weight should now be on the back foot with a high back lift. Hit the ball either level or just behind eye level. This depends upon where the batsman wishes to hit the ball – i.e. in front or behind square.

- It is a cross-batted shot with the arms fully extended and a full follow-through of the bat. The batsman can either hit the ball down with a high to low movement or, if there is an inner ring of fielders, it is possible to bring the bat up and under the ball to elevate the ball over the ring into the air.

Robin Smith's cut shot was built on a firm base that gave him excellent balance.

Problems and fixes

- *The ball keeps going in the air.* The bottom hand may be too strong causing the bat to come from under the ball rather than from high to low. If the batsman is leaning back on the shot the bat may be coming up under the ball on impact.

- *Top-edging the ball.* The ball may be too close to the body to play the shot. If the batsman is unable to free the arms then it is the wrong shot selection.

- *The bounce of the wicket is inconsistent.* This is a dangerous shot to play on a wicket offering variable bounce. This could result in either a top edge going in the air or a bottom edge going into the stumps.

- *Not in control of the shot.* If the batsman doesn't get back and across sufficiently, they could end up being cramped for room, resulting in stepping away with the left leg to the leg side to try and create more power. This means the eyes aren't over the line of the ball, increasing the chances the batsman will be caught behind or close into the wicket.

Practice drill

- Place a batting tee on a stump with a tennis ball on top in the correct position to play the shot. The batsman steps back and across and plays the shot.
- Introduce bounce feeds and then move on to the bowling machine.

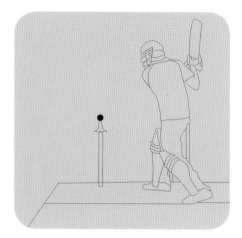

OTHER SHOTS

Leg-glance (see diagram on page 81)

What it is

Not every run has to be scored by a thumping cut or a beautiful drive. Often the key to building a big total is picking up singles or twos, especially early in the innings as the batsman gets used to the pace of the pitch.

One of the easiest ways to do this is by taking advantage of any scoring opportunities when the bowler strays onto the pads. The leg-glance is a wristy stroke with the purpose of picking up those ones and twos, although there is the chance of a boundary if timed well. Left-handers are traditionally very strong in this area as the right-arm bowlers often struggle to adjust to the new angle.

When to play it

This is played to a full-length delivery on the line of leg-stump or going down the leg-side, and normally turned behind square on the leg-side.

How to play it

- Only take a small step forwards with the left foot slightly inside the line of the ball.

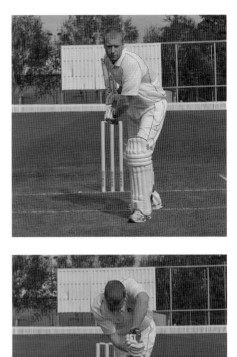

- The batsman's head should be in the line of the ball and just over the front foot.

- As the ball arrives, the batsman should play it just in front of them and allow their wrists to rotate towards the leg-side. Again, this is a touch shot played with soft hands; the batsman is using the pace on the delivery.

Batsman to study

ALASTAIR COOK (England 2006–)
Cook's strength when playing this stroke is watching the ball closely and waiting until the last possible moment before turning his wrists to time the ball off his pads.

Alastair Cook is excellent off his legs – a key scoring area for all left-handers.

Problems and fixes

- *Turning the wrists too early.* This can result in a leading edge and a probable catch. Wait until the last possible moment before turning the wrists.

- *Head falling off-side of the ball.* If this is happening then balance becomes an issue. The batsman will fall over to the off-side of the ball and probably fall out of the crease. If the wicket-keeper is stood up to the stumps then the batsman might be out-stumped, while they are also an LBW candidate if they miss the ball.

Practice drill

- It would be best to use the bowling machine due to the accuracy it gives, otherwise face underarm throws, and try and turn the ball towards a specified target on the leg-side.

Back foot leg-glance (see diagram on page 81)

What it is

The back foot version of the leg-glance, it's a shot used by batsmen to relieve the pressure if a bowler is bowling short at their body.

When to play it

This shot is played to a back of a length delivery bouncing up between thigh and rib height on the line of the leg-stump.

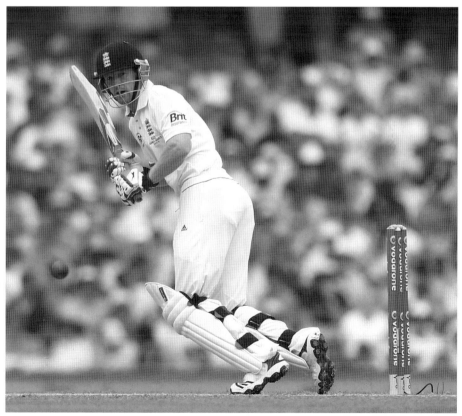

Paul Collingwood's nurdle off his hips became his trademark shot.

How to play it

- Take the head and shoulder to the line of the ball. The right foot goes back and across with toes pointing to extra cover.

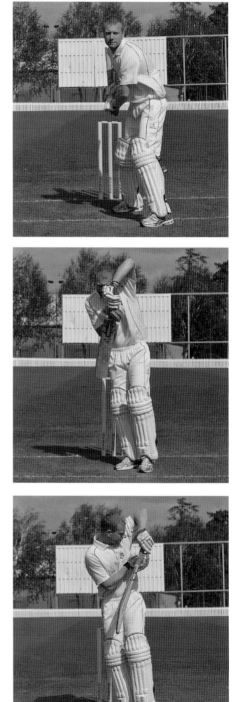

- Draw the left foot back so it is close to the back foot. The batsman is now in a more open body position.

- The batsman will need to play the ball as late as possible with their hands, turning the bat face to the leg-side at the last moment. Remember this is a touch shot. Let the pace of the ball do the work.

PAUL COLLINGWOOD (England 2004–2011)
Collingwood became synonymous with defiant rearguards during his England career. He was a batsman who understood his technique and its limitations perfectly and based his scoring areas around this knowledge. The back foot leg-glance became a reliable scoring area under pressure.

Problems and fixes

- *The back foot stays side-on.* This makes it very difficult to play the shot as the bat pathway has to come across the body in a stabbing motion. Make sure the back foot is pointing down the wicket.

- *Head and eye position not forward and level with the ball.* The batsman might turn the bat face too early resulting in a leading edge.

Practice drill

- As for the front foot leg-glance use either 'throw downs' or the bowling machine.

Late cut (see diagram on page 81)

What it is

Attempted by many, perfected by few – the late cut is the ultimate touch shot, the sign of a batsman in total control. To play it properly the batsman should be sure of the pace and bounce of the ball, waiting until the last possible moment before deflecting it very fine behind square on the off-side. Beware the perils – too fine a contact and the keeper has an easy catch behind the stumps. This is a useful shot when the fielding side has no fielders behind square on the off-side.

When to play it

The late cut shot is played to a good length delivery just outside the line of the off-stump against a spin or medium-paced bowler. It is a touch shot. The batsman uses the pace of the ball to steer it delicately very fine between first and second slip.

How to play it

- Bending the knees, take the back foot back and across to finish just inside the line of the ball.

- Turn the left shoulder to the line of the ball and keep the eyes locked on to it.

- Allow the ball to go past the body. Just before it reaches the wicket-keeper's gloves, dab at the ball with an open face of the bat. Run it down to the third man area.

MAHELA JAYAWARDENE (Sri Lanka 1997–)
A hallmark of Jayawardene's game is the time he has to play each shot. He waits until the last possible moment before flicking the ball down to third man just as it is entering the wicket-keeper's gloves.

Problems and fixes

- *Head back on the shot.* This will lead to a lack of control and power, and a potential catch behind the wicket. Get right over the ball.

- *Low pick-up and dominant bottom hand.* This will mean a loss of power and the bat face closing early, which could lead to a top edge.

Practice drill

- Tennis ball feeds from 10 metres thrown by the coach on a good length outside the off-stump. A little bit of pace on the ball is necessary for the shot to be played at its best.
- Move on to the bowling machine and introduce a wicket-keeper. The batsman can then practise almost taking the ball out of the wicket-keeper's hands.

Move down the wicket for lofted drive (see diagram on page 81)
What it is
Using their feet against the spinner or even the quicker bowler is an excellent way for the batsman to disrupt their rhythm and earn themself more bad balls to score against. But be careful (see playing spin, page 104).

When to play it
This strategy is usually used to a good length delivery bowled by a spinner or medium-paced bowler. Remember not to step down until after the bowler has bowled.

IAN BELL (England 2004–)
As Bell's game has improved, so has his foot movement to the spinners. Decisive foot movement is a trademark of a player who believes in their own ability.

Ian Bell steps down the pitch to drive with a flourish during the 2010–11 Ashes.

How to play it

There are two main ways of coming down the wicket.

- **The shimmy** – head and left shoulder lead with a big left foot stride straight. The right foot then comes up alongside the left leg and leg-side of the front leg. Head and shoulder then move to the line of the ball, with the legs following to help establish a solid base for striking.

- **The clogg** – as above, except that both feet continue on the same line. The back foot almost clips the front foot as the batsman advances.

- The shimmy allows the batsman to come further down the wicket. Whichever the batsman selects, they should keep their eyes level throughout.
- Once a technique has been selected, don't over-hit. Make impact just after the ball has bounced with the front leg bent and head level with the front foot.
- The batsman should allow their front elbow to control the shot then engage the bottom hand for power. They should look to get under the ball for elevation but not lean too far back, making sure their weight is evenly distributed. The ideal is to hit the ball one bounce for a four. This will maintain the shape of the shot and it will go a long way. The batsman should allow a full follow-through of the hands.
- To hit along the ground, simply impact on the half volley as described in straight drives, keeping the head over the ball.
- Lastly, as the batsman comes down the wicket, the ball may not be there to attack. Don't be afraid to readjust and play a defensive shot to avoid being stumped or bowled.

Problems and fixes

- *First step too small.* This will mean the batsman will struggle to get to the pitch of the ball. Be decisive with the first stride.

- *Weight back on the shot.* This will cause the ball to go straight up in the air. Get over the ball.

- *Bottom hand too dominant.* This will cause a loss of the control of the front elbow. The bat face closes and comes across the ball causing a slice or a drag to the leg-side.

- *Playing around the left leg.* If the first movement is too far to the off-side the batsman cannot get their head back into the line of the ball.

Practice drills

- Drop-feed with tennis balls. Player rehearses the shot and then indicates where they would like the ball dropped. The player calls drop when they are ready and practises lofted and straight drives.
- Place cones on the line of middle-and-off stumps to encourage and cement the practice of coming down the wicket straight. The first movement should be led by head and shoulder, with the left shoulder pointing to where the line of the ball is coming from.

- The coach throws tennis balls from 22 yards. The batsman comes down the wicket and practises the stroke including hitting over extra cover. The coach can call whether they are delivering a lofted or straight drive as they throw.

EXPERT COACHING TIP

If the batsman wants to improve their power hitting they should stick to these basic principles:

- Stay still
- Have a solid base
- Hit straight through the line

Front foot press to spin

What it is

The forward press is a way for the batsman to get under the flight of a spinning delivery, and give the bowler the impression they are about to advance down the wicket.

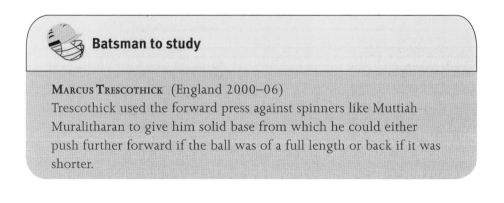

Batsman to study

MARCUS TRESCOTHICK (England 2000–06)
Trescothick used the forward press against spinners like Muttiah Muralitharan to give him solid base from which he could either push further forward if the ball was of a full length or back if it was shorter.

When and how to do it

- Just before the bowler delivers, the batsman takes a small step forwards with their left leg and bends both knees – this lowers their head and body position.

- This can deceive the bowler into thinking the batsman is about to come down the wicket. One of the spinner's main weapons is to get the ball above the batsman's eyeline to deceive them in the flight. By lowering the body, the eyes will now stay under the flight of the ball, making it a lot easier to follow the ball's path. For the batsman this is negated by having a lower starting position, as the eyes stay under the flight of the ball throughout its delivery.
- From the press position, batsmen tend to transfer their weight backwards or forwards to attack or defend. The batsman is in a position for a number of sweep shots as the stance is a lot lower than usual.

Problems and fixes

- *If the press is too big this makes it very difficult to get down the pitch.* If the batsman has a different trigger for pace bowling it is important that they practise both so that one does not encroach on the other.

- *The batsman's press goes towards the off-stump.* They may find themself becoming blocked off. Consequently they would have to play around their front leg, limiting their options and becoming prone to a possible LBW.

Practice drill

- Like trigger movements, this is a matter of perfecting timing. Use a similar drill.

SWEEP SHOTS

The sweep shot is normally played against the spinner, to a ball that is not full enough to drive, but can still be reached on the half-volley by the batsman as they go down on one knee. The name of the shot is taken from the sweeping motion the batsman should make to connect with the ball from this position.

The sweep is often used by batsmen looking to rotate the strike and manipulate the field against the spinners, normally to balls pitching on or outside leg-stump. It is a risky shot as, once committed to the stroke, the batsman is at the mercy of any unpredictable bounce, which might lead to a top-edge and a catch. There is also the possibility of an LBW decision if the batsman fails to make contact with the ball, and this might happen if the ball is too full or too short.

When played well, the sweep is an extremely effective way of upsetting the bowler's rhythm, particularly in limited-overs cricket where the need to score is greater, but many coaches prefer to teach batsman to play straight and leave the sweep alone.

The sweep shot and its exciting, if often unorthodox, variations have become increasingly prevalent as batsmen have turned to innovation as a means of opening up new scoring areas in Twenty20 cricket and one-day cricket. If the opposition are having to put fielders where the batsman is sweeping and reverse-sweeping, then there will be holes somewhere else.

While it's always good to try and learn new skills in the nets, be aware that the players who are using these shots on television have been practising them hard for years.

Orthodox sweep

What it is

This is used more on a turning pitch when it may be difficult to come down the wicket. The stroke is used to disrupt the length of the spin bowler. It is important to be aware of which way the bowler is spinning the ball, how much they are spinning it, and how much bounce they are generating. The batsman should also watch the spinner to see if they have a variation delivery that might deceive the batsman in the flight.

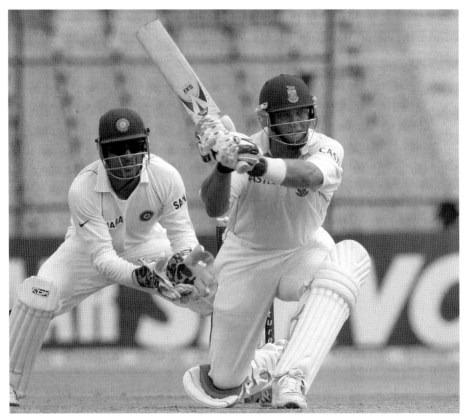

Jacques Kallis is a masterful manipulator of slow bowling.

When to play it

The sweep is played against a spin bowler when the ball is bowled on a good length. The line of the delivery is usually middle-and-leg stump or going down the leg-side.

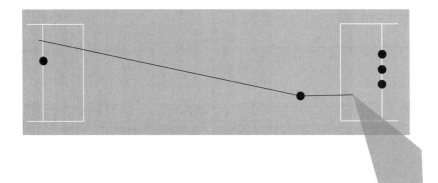

How to play it

- Take a comfortable stride forward to the line of the ball. The front leg bends and the back knee sinks onto the ground. The back leg should be off-side of the front knee to help establish a solid base. Get low to the ball.

- The batsman should have high hands and keep their head position just over the front knee on impact. The arms should be fully extended with the bat staying parallel to the ground.

- Roll the wrists on impact and keep the head and eyes watching the ball even after playing the shot.

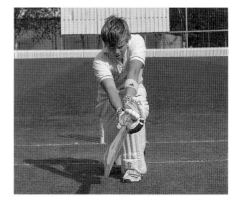

JACQUES KALLIS (South Africa 1995–)
Kallis maintains the perfect head position while sweeping, allowing
him to retain as much control over a difficult shot as possible.

Problems and fixes

- *Head position is back behind the front knee.* The batsman must correct their balance
  and get their head forward otherwise they will lose power and control in the
  shot.

- *The bat pathway is too steep.* Top-edges are inevitable if the bat is brought down
  too sharply. Remember it is called a sweep, not a chop.

- *Feet are in a straight line.* This will affect the balance badly. If the batsman's base is
  not solid, there will be no power in the shot, and no control, as above.

Practice drill

- Get down into the sweep position and establish a strong, consistent base. Hit
  tennis balls off a batting tee. Bobble-feeds in same position.

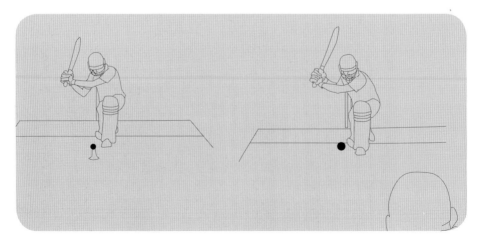

- Place a cone alongside the length that the batsman is going to sweep. The
  coach stands six metres away and underarms the ball on to the spot. Practise
  from the usual position. Move on to the bowling machine.

SCORING AREAS

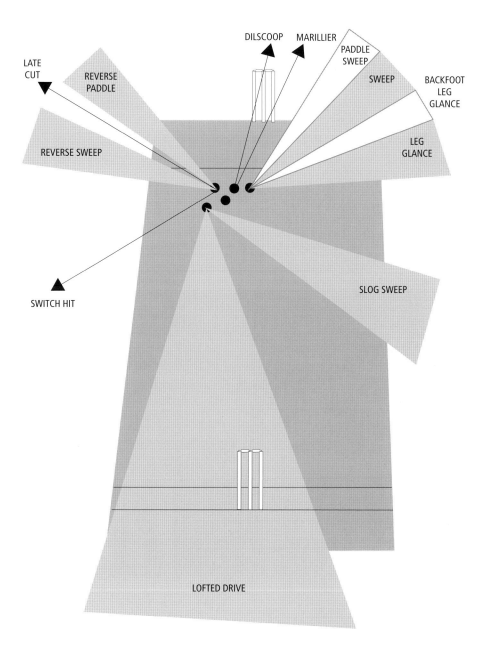

DILSCOOP MARILLIER

PADDLE
SWEEP

LATE
CUT

REVERSE
PADDLE

SWEEP

BACKFOOT
LEG
GLANCE

REVERSE SWEEP

LEG
GLANCE

SLOG SWEEP

SWITCH HIT

LOFTED DRIVE

Paddle sweep (see diagram on page 81)

What it is

The batsman uses the pace on the ball to guide it fine on the leg-side.

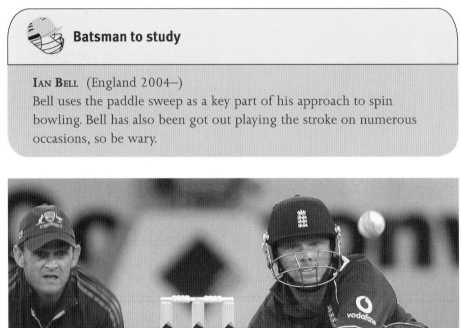

Batsman to study

IAN BELL (England 2004–)

Bell uses the paddle sweep as a key part of his approach to spin bowling. Bell has also been got out playing the stroke on numerous occasions, so be wary.

It's worth noting how intently England's Ian Bell is watching the ball before this paddle sweep.

When to play it

As with the orthodox sweep shot, this is played to a full spinning delivery, normally pitching on or leg-side of middle stump.

How to play it

- Exactly the same technique as the orthodox sweep shot. The main difference is that the batsman's arms don't need to be fully extended.

- Draw the arms back towards the body; allow the back of the bat to rest on the ground and tilt the face of the bat to the angle the batsman wants the ball to go in.

- This shot is about manipulation. The batsman is not hitting the ball; they are using the pace of the ball to guide it, usually very fine on the leg-side. If they have gone down to the orthodox sweep shot and have misjudged the length as a lot fuller, this shot can potentially get them out of trouble.

Practice drill

- Get the coach to throw balls with a bit of pace on them, and practise working on the angles of the sweep.

Fender gave some amusement by hitting Armstrong back-handed on the off-side for a couple.

PELHAM WARNER, PERHAPS RECORDING THE FIRST REVERSE SWEEP, FROM PERCY FENDER IN HIS REPORT IN THE CRICKETER ON THE OLD TRAFFORD TEST OF 1921 BETWEEN ENGLAND AND AUSTRALIA

Reverse sweep (see diagram on page 81)

What it is

A cross-batted shot to the spin bowler, essentially the reverse of the orthodox sweep, but played with the same grip. This is used by batsmen to manipulate field placements.

Eoin Morgan's extraordinary dexterity on display for England against Pakistan.

When to play it

This shot is normally determined by the field setting and the line the spinner is adopting. The point is to manipulate the ball to force the opposition to plug the gap and then open up more conventional areas to score in.

How to play it

- It is basically the mirror image of sweeping left-handed except the batsman's hands change from top to bottom (not by taking the hands off the bat). The right leg leads and the left knee should neither bend nor be placed on the ground.

- Getting into position quickly is essential. The batsman is now left-handed, so the bottom hand is on top of the bat and the top hand is on the bottom with the bat face turning to the off-side.

- Execute the shot as if playing a left-handed sweep.

Batsman to study

EOIN MORGAN (England 2009–)
Morgan's ability to react late to deliveries makes him a nightmare to bowl against. His ability to combine strike-rotation with a host of improvised shots and big hitting makes him one of the most exciting players in world cricket.

Problems and fixes
- *Moving too early.* This is a pre-meditated shot but don't go too early, as the bowler will spot the movement and bowl a flatter delivery and this will be more difficult to hit.

- *Misjudging length.* This will make the batsman an LBW candidate. The batsman should watch the ball out of the hand closely until it hits the bat.

Practice drill
- Hit tennis balls off a cone to practise the basic movements.
- Bowling machine work or throw downs working on authentic or reverse sweep. Use cones as targets in the field to aim towards to practise field-manipulation.

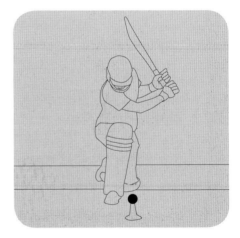

I have thumbed through the MCC coaching manual and found that no such stroke exists.
PETER MAY, CHAIRMAN OF SELECTORS, AFTER OBSERVING IAN BOTHAM PLAY A REVERSE SWEEP, 1985

Reverse paddle (see diagram on page 81)

What it is

The reverse paddle is a finer version of the reverse sweep, only accessible to most dextrous of players.

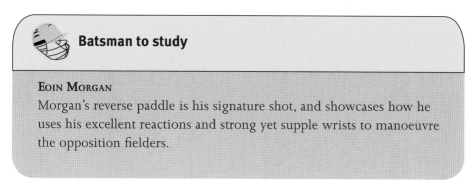

Batsman to study

EOIN MORGAN

Morgan's reverse paddle is his signature shot, and showcases how he uses his excellent reactions and strong yet supple wrists to manoeuvre the opposition fielders.

When to play it

This shot needs to be played to a full ball from the spinner with pace on it, bowled on or around off-stump.

How to play it

- As with the orthodox sweep, establish a solid base.

- Turn the bat in the hands. Keep the hands the same way on the handle.

- Keep the hands high, and then apply the same motion as for the orthodox sweep. Move the hands from high to low, and be careful not to jab at the ball.

- Roll the hands on the bat depending on where the batsman wants the ball to go.

Slog sweep (see diagram on page 81)

What it is

A more aggressive shot from the same base as the orthodox sweep.

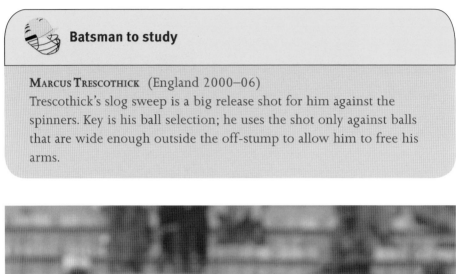

Batsman to study

MARCUS TRESCOTHICK (England 2000–06)

Trescothick's slog sweep is a big release shot for him against the spinners. Key is his ball selection; he uses the shot only against balls that are wide enough outside the off-stump to allow him to free his arms.

Marcus Trescothick's command of the slog sweep gives him an extra attacking option against slow bowling.

When to play it

This shot is played to a length delivery from a spinner or gentle medium pace bowler. The objective is to disrupt the bowler and manipulate the field, showing aggressive intent and possibly removing close fielders.

How to play it

- The technique is similar to the orthodox sweep except the batsman is required to get their left leg away from the line of the ball.

- The batsman can then extend their arms to get under the ball. This allows for elevation and power in the shot possibly resulting in a four or a six. Look for width outside the off-stump.

Problems and fixes

- *Head back on the shot – no power.* Could lead to a top edge and being caught out.

- *Low pick up and a dominant bottom hand.* This means a loss of power and the bat face closing early. This could lead to a top edge.

Practice drill

- Use tennis ball feeds from a distance of six metres. Practise hitting the ball in the air and along the ground.

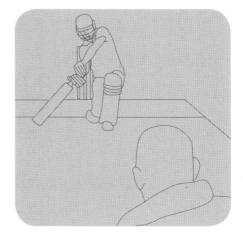

OTHER VARIATION SHOTS

Switch-hit (see diagram on page 81)

What it is

This was a shot first seen in 2008 when Kevin Pietersen unleashed it on New Zealand. It takes the reverse sweep a stage further, with the aim of hitting the ball for six on the off-side to the right-hander, or the leg-side of the new left-handed stance. It is very much a shot for a desperate or luxury situation, and most likely to be seen in one-day or Twenty20 cricket.

When to play it

When the team is in need of quick runs and the field is out on the leg-side boundary. This is a shot that is easier to attempt against medium pacers or spin bowlers, particularly if they are bowling very straight to a packed leg-side field.

How to play it

- As the bowler is running in the batsman switches their hands and feet around to that of a left-hander's grip and stance.

- The batsman must make sure they still have time to get set with a solid base. The bowler will see the early move but that cannot be helped, it is important to be in the best possible position to play the shot. The batsman must decide whether to hit the ball along the floor or in the air.

- As with a slog sweep or more orthodox shots, it is important to get a good back-lift in, and to try not to hit the ball too hard.

- Rotate the hips through the ball and flick the wrists to give the shot extra power.

EXPERT COACHING TIP

Pietersen said of the shot after that New Zealand game, 'I have spent many hours in the nets working on it'. This is proof that the reason the pros can play such unorthodox shots is because they spend a lot of time practising their skills. Do the same before you try new shots in a match.

Kevin Pietersen invents a new shot against New Zealand in 2009.

The Marillier (see diagram on page 81)
What it is
The Marillier is another innovative shot, named after the Zimbabwean Doug Marillier, who pioneered the shot against Australia in 2001. Marillier invented the shot as a way to convert yorkers into full-tosses at the end of a limited-overs innings. It involved stepping across his stumps and using the bat as a ramp to lift the ball on the full over a short fine-leg fielder.

When to play it
Marillier first used the stroke when Zimbabwe played Australia in a one-day international and Glenn McGrath was bowling full at the base of off-stump, with fine-leg up in the ring.

How to play it
*   As the bowler is about to deliver the ball, the batsman should step forward and across the stumps so they are standing outside off-stump just outside the crease.

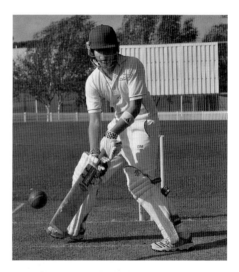

*   If the ball is full, bend the front knee and get low, using the face of the bat to scoop the ball over the fielder at short fine leg.

*   The batsman should make sure they get their head out of the way, so that they do not get hit by the ball in the process of trying to flick it round the corner.

The Dilscoop (see diagram on page 81)

What it is

The Dilscoop is a very, very, high-risk shot, for the batsman's own safety as much as their wicket. It is the Sri Lankan opening batsman Tillekeratne Dilshan's interpretation of Marillier's shot. Dilshan also uses the bat as a ramp, but in more orthodox, if alarming fashion, as he seeks to scoop a straight, good length delivery from a seamer over the head of himself and the wicket-keeper.

When to play it

Dilshan favours straight, good length deliveries from medium pace or quicker bowlers, where he can use the pace on the ball. He favours the shot particularly against left-arm seamers when he is comfortable that the ball is coming across him. It's a shot that is of most use when the field is up at the beginning or the end of the innings. Dilshan has said he only uses the shot when his eye is in.

How to play it

- When the batsman sees that the ball is the right length to play the shot, they should get down on one knee as though going to sweep the ball. Instead of taking the hands high as they would for a sweep, keep them low.

- As the ball approaches, the batsman should get their head and eyes down and level with the ball, and at the last minute use the bat to scoop it up over the head and the wicket-keeper.

- It is vital for the batsman's safety that they watch the ball right until it hits the bat.

Practice drill

- The coach throws underarm balls with a tennis ball. The batsman should practise getting on one knee, making sure they get the right head position and most of all are watching the ball until they connect with it. Only when the batsman has mastered this should they move on to a cricket ball, and eventually a bowling machine.

THE ADVANCED STAGES

3.

TACTICS

So those are the shots. Among them is everything the batsman needs to succeed. But there's much more to batting than waving a bat around. Unless we're talking about an opener, it's quite likely that every time a batsman goes to the wicket it will be a slightly different situation, a slightly different test of technique and mind. How a batsman reacts to these different situations and applies their technique accordingly determines what level they will reach.

Once a batsman reaches a certain technical level the game is largely played in the mind. Which balls do I hit? What shot do I play to them? Am I nervous facing this bowler? Am I under pressure to score runs? Somehow the batsman must push all these questions to one side and just worry about hitting the ball.

This chapter aims to help a player get the best out of their batting, to understand their game better than others, and to become the person that every opposition team wants to see the back of.

Pre-match routine

While routine isn't essential to scoring lots of runs, it can help to focus the mind for the task ahead. The player should think back to previous dismissals they have had, and how many times they've arrived at the wicket not mentally prepared to bat.

Walk out to the pitch before the match starts. Stand at both ends and go through a simple checklist:

- How big is the boundary? Is it shorter on one side?
- What are the wind conditions? Is it helpful for hitting towards the short boundary? Or unhelpful for hitting towards the long boundary?

- What type of wicket is it? (Is it green? Seamer friendly? Or a used wicket, which would be helpful to spinners?)
- Does the pitch slope? If so, does it affect the stance?

This simple list has already given the batsman a big head-start in formulating their game plan for the match ahead.

Fitness and nutrition

Fitness and diet

The higher level a batsman is playing at, the more important their fitness and diet, especially if they intend to bat for long periods. Every person has different requirements, so it is recommended that each player speaks to an expert who can give them the best dietary advice and fitness routine to suit them personally.

Fluids

If the batsman is going to bat for a long time they may get dehydrated so they should take plenty of fluids on board before and during their innings. This is even more important when they know they are likely to be batting in hot conditions.

Reading the pitch

Being able to look at the surface of the pitch and understand how it might play and what sort of total may be obtained is a great asset for any batsman. The following provides a rough guide of what to look for. The best advice is for the batsman to judge with their own eyes – the batsman should watch what happens to other batsmen on the pitch and try and anticipate how they might tailor their own game to the surface.

Flat surface/straw-like grass colour This should be even. A consistently paced pitch is ideal for batting. There should be little or no seam movement or spin in the early stages.

Green (plenty of grass) This indicates moisture in the grass which will aid seam movement. The batsmen should be watchful against the new ball. As the wicket is green the ball won't lose its shine so swing bowling may also be of concern. The ball is unlikely to spin a great deal.

Cracked surfaces This will encourage uneven bounce. All cross-batted shots will be risky. Batsmen will need to be very watchful and should look to play straight.

Dry pitch/dusty used surface Spin bowlers will be a danger, meaning coming down the pitch will be difficult. If the surface is loose, then a seam bowler who bowls cutters will get the ball to bite and spit.

Drying out/damp surface This should favour bowlers bowling seam or cutters as the seam will dig in to the damp wicket. Balls may behave inconsistently – some will stop on the batsman and some will climb. It is very difficult to bat fluently on this type of surface. Some consider attack is the best option, a quick 30 or 40 could make all the difference.

Uneven surface (corrugated) The high spots will be easily visible – a brown colour or bare patch where the mower has scalped the surface. The lower parts will be green and soft to the touch as the roller has not touched them due to the undulations. When the ball hits an up-slope it will climb and bounce higher than normal; when it hits a down-slope, it will skid on and keep low. When it hits the softer, green areas the seam will dig in and create variable bounce. On pitches like this it is best to have an attacking frame of mind as survival will be difficult.

> **The best technique in the world is no good if you're backing away to square leg.**
> Geoff Boycott, coaching England's batsmen on attributes needed to face West Indies in 1989

Playing pace

Every batsman should be looking to develop their game in preparation for a higher level of cricket against pace bowling. To do that the batsman must develop a game plan and an understanding of their strengths and weaknesses.

Facing genuine pace bowling is as hard as it gets in cricket, but it's worth remembering that with the extra pace on the ball it can go a lot quicker to the boundary. Fast bowlers thrive on visible weakness, but it's a tough and demanding thing to do, and can lead to more scoring opportunities – it's easier than one might think to get on top of a misfiring quick.

If the batsman is brave, confident and looks to score when possible, they'll soon find fast bowling gets easier and easier to face.

The batsman should follow the advice below to give themself the best chance of success.

- Speed of thought and decision-making are crucial against quick bowling.
- When playing quick bowlers a batsman's foot movements are generally smaller and quicker. The batsman will need to play the ball closer to their body. Do not get drawn into playing away from the eye-line or body.
- The batsman should predetermine a strategy against the short-pitched delivery. Are they pulling/hooking/cutting/evading or simply defending and picking up singles?
- What type of wicket is it? If the surface is hard and has an even grass covering (not overly green), the batsman can assume that the bounce of the ball will be even and consistent. This allows them to play the cross-batted shots with confidence.
- The batsman should appear to thrive with the challenge, look the bowler in the eye and appear confident, even giving them a little smile. This suggests that the batsman is comfortable and at ease with whatever they have to face. Show courage. From time to time a batsman will take a few hits but they must shrug it off, smile and prepare for the next delivery. It is important not to show pain even if it hurts. If the bowler or fielders start to give the batsman verbal abuse, they must ignore them. They are trying to intimidate the batsman and break their concentration. Again the batsman should not get drawn into it; smile and focus on batting. They will soon be quiet when they realise they are not getting a reaction.
- Another useful tip when playing fast bowlers is to try to get some help from what the bowler does. Which side of the ball is the shiny one as they run in and at what angle is the seam pointing? How fast are they running in – a quicker run up than usual indicates either a short delivery or faster deliver. The height of release is also worth looking out for – if the bowler drops down early it is usually a sign of a shorter delivery.

Don't like quick bowling? Problem solved
As schoolboys develop, there comes an age when they have to face up to fast bowling and short-pitched deliveries. There are very few cricketers, up to and including the elite level, that actually enjoy facing short-pitched (bouncer) bowling.

Many schoolboy cricketers are troubled by the fear of getting hit. This fear often drives the batsman back – meaning that at point of delivery the set-up (stance) and weight (head position) moves to level or over the back foot, when it should be just behind the front foot. This makes it impossible to move and the batsman becomes a sitting target for the short-pitched delivery.

A player may also have taken a blow to the helmet or upper body and lost their confidence dealing with the short ball. In either case, at some point down the line the batsman will have to face up to their demons.

To deal with the situation the batsman should go back to basics. Tennis ball feeds – working on defence – pull shots and evasion. Focus on the importance of being able to move in the crease. The batsman should maintain a neutral head position prior to delivery at all times. The coach can now ramp up the drills, including throw-downs and the bowling machine. The batsman should focus on defending and evasion. Leave the pull/hook shots alone until confidence and technique are fully restored.

Down the line the batsman will have to face short deliveries again. Start in the nets: a useful tip is to either evade the bouncer or play the ball down for a single. It is much easier playing the quick bowler from the non-striker's end. If a batsman plays the short ball well, the bowler will soon leave them alone and try another mode of dismissal.

Practice drills against pace bowling

The coach throws or bowls cricket balls from a distance of 12–14 metres away. Start with full or 'back of a length' deliveries. This will encourage speed of movement and mind. It is important that the batsman does not guess. Move on to the bowling machine, crank up the machine's pace and develop techniques against pace (pull/cut/hook/evade/defence).

Playing swing bowling

For a long time the swinging ball filled me with the fear of God.
COLIN COWDREY, ENGLAND BATSMAN, ON HIS EARLY STRUGGLES AT KENT

Good swing bowling is a dramatic skill to watch – a bowler who has the ability to curve the ball towards or away from a batsman is always going to cause problems. That said, it's another difficult thing to get right, so a batsman should be wary but not negative when facing it. The swing bowler will always be looking to pitch the ball up so when it doesn't swing or they don't quite get it right, there will be opportunities to score.

Bowler's action and how they are likely to swing it
What should you look for in a bowler's action to see which way they might be looking to swing the ball? As a general rule this is what you might expect:
- **Side-on** bowlers tend to bowl **out-swing**.
- **Chest/front-on** bowlers tend to bowl **in-swing**.
- The **position of the bowler's wrist on release:** 11 o'clock in-swing; 1 o'clock out-swing.
- If the bowler falls away to the offside early with their head, the ball can only swing in.
- If the bowler pulls their front arm/shoulder down quickly, it tends to lead to a short ball.

Some bowlers will swing the ball straight out of their hand, some will move it much later. Late swing can be very difficult to play, so watch the ball carefully. Similarly, if a bowler is moving the ball off the seam, the batsman should look to follow the rules below:
- Focus on the ball in the bowler's hand; which side of the ball is shiny and at what position is the seam pointing? This can give an early signal as to which way the ball may swing.
- A simple rule to follow is to hit the ball in the direction of the swing. Hit an out-swing bowler mainly through the off-side and an in-swing bowler through the leg-side. If the batsman plays against the swing it can encourage leading edges (playing out-swing bowlers into the leg-side) or inside edges and being bowled (driving in-swing bowlers through the off-side).

- It is important for the batsman to know where their off-stump is when facing out-swing bowlers. Many batsmen follow the ball and end up playing at deliveries that they could have left with an open-faced bat, which can result in edging the ball behind.
- Try to work out if the swing bowler has a variation. For example, if an out-swing bowler cannot move it back in towards the stumps then it is safe to leave a ball that pitches just outside the off-stump.
- The batsman should not commit early to an in-swing bowler do not commit early as they will end up playing around the front pad. If the batsman misses, then LBW is a strong possibility.
- Once technique is focussed upon, the batsman can explore batting outside of their crease (providing the wicket-keeper is stood back). This can disrupt the bowler's length and also negate any late swing.

Graham Thorpe on counter-attacking

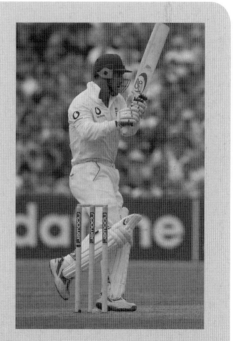

If you have to up your game and fire a few bullets back to a bowler who's bowling very well, you again have to work out the risk factor in terms of counter-attacking. But if that comes off a few times for you, it gives you a real belief that you can take the attack to the opposition bowlers.

Likewise, sometimes when there's a really good spell being bowled at you, you also have to know when to dig in. You might have to bat for an hour for not many runs. What's important is the ability to adapt – to sense the situation and play either way.

Graham Thorpe played 100 Tests for England between 1993 and 2005. This interview originally appeared in the Wisden Cricketer

Playing spin

The one and only way to foil a spin attack is by quick footwork, aggression and the spirit of adventure.
CHARLIE MACARTNEY, HEADINGLEY TEST, ENGLAND VS AUSTRALIA, 1938

Playing spin seems to have a stigma attached for English batsmen, and especially young batsmen. Maybe it's the element of risk involved in playing aggressively, that the batsman has to put the pace on the ball or that the ball goes up above the batsman's eye-line. Either way, the batsman should think positively, and not worry if their ambition occasionally gets them out.

Batsmen from other countries, particularly those from India, Sri Lanka, Pakistan and Bangladesh who have grown up on turning sub-continental surfaces, are very comfortable in using their feet to get to the pitch of the ball. Those from South Africa and Australia, who traditionally place emphasis on an aggressive approach, will also make an effort to confront the spinner early in their spell.

Mushtaq Ahmed on mistakes batsmen make against spin

Sometimes batsmen don't respect the spinners enough. They have a lot of things going on in their mind and they often try to play lots of shots. That's a way of making more mistakes. Batsmen take risks against spin they wouldn't take against seamers, and in doing so they can lose control.

Mushtaq Ahmed played 52 Tests for Pakistan

When the former South African batsman Darryl Cullinan was coaching age-group sides at Kent he instructed the top-order batsmen he was coaching to try to hit the off-spinner over the top on a good batting pitch within the first three balls of their spell. Cullinan didn't care if the batsman got out (within reason), as long as they were approaching the situation with the right mindset and trying to hit straight with the appropriate shot selection.

While it appears to differ from the advice given by Mushtaq Ahmed above, Cullinan's point was that the needs of the team were more important than the individual batsman – in this instance, not to let the spinner settle into a spell and slow down the run rate. This tactic is ultra positive and potentially risky, particularly, for example, on a pitch offering sharp turn, but is instructive of the positive mindset that should be the priority of the individual batsman and the team against spin bowling. For less experienced players we would recommend taking a couple of balls to see what the spinner is doing.

Playing spin on a flat wicket

- The batsman's plan, as always, should be to play to their strengths.
- Set up slightly deeper in the crease as the wicket-keeper will be up to the stumps and looking for any stumping opportunities.
- The batsman should always try to be positive and dominate, especially when conditions are in the batsman's favour. Any type of bowler needs time to settle into a rhythm. It is important the batsman takes control. On a wicket offering little or no spin, the batsman should take the opportunity to get down the wicket and put the spinner on the back foot early in their spell.
- Being positive is not all about the big shots. Look to manipulate the ball into gaps. Cricket is like chess, the batsman has to outwit and stay ahead of the bowler. Manipulating the ball results in field-changes, which asserts the batsman's control. On a non-turning surface the batsman's scoring arc becomes much bigger to the spinner.
- When facing the left-arm orthodox or the leg-spinner the batsman should look to hit on the off-side. If the pitch is particularly flat, the batsman can expand their shot selection to include the leg-side.

Playing spin on a turning wicket

- A right-hander facing an off-spinner on a turning pitch should consider a number of problems. With the ball turning into them, playing through the off-side can be dangerous, as can coming down the wicket. Look to hit the off-spinner with the spin, so anywhere from fine leg to mid-on. The sweep shot also becomes a good option, if the batsman judges the length and line of the ball carefully. The batsman will tend to hit more with the spin into the leg-side.
- The left-arm orthodox and leg-spinner pose different problems on a turning wicket, with the ball turning away from the right-hander. If the batsman comes down the wicket they must get to the pitch of the ball. If they do not, the ball will spin past the outside edge and there is a risk they will be bowled or stumped. The primary tactic should be to try to hit the ball in the direction it spins. Any loose deliveries should be punished. If gaps are left on the leg-side, the batsman may consider playing through that area but be wary of getting a leading edge.
- Left-handers should apply the same principles in reverse, i.e. treat a left-arm orthodox or leg-spinner as a right-hander would an off-spinner, and an off-spinner as a right-hander would a left-arm orthodox.

Scoring runs

Every batsman aims to score runs. It doesn't have to be complicated – many batsmen are successful because they're good at simplifying that aim in their mind.

There are many high-scoring club and professional batsmen who get by on perfecting and relying on just three or four shots. They may still work on other shots but their main focus is on their 'bankers'. A batsman should stick to maybe their best two or three shots i.e. cover drive, square cut. Remember to avoid being tempted or made to play risky shots.

Be positive in attack or defence. A batsman is there to score runs. When the batsman attacks, they must do it decisively. When they defend, they must remember they are defending so that they are still there to attack the next ball, or because the team needs them to survive.

Rotation of the strike is important. Think every ball has a number – a six, four, three, two or one. If it is a good delivery try to manoeuvre the ball for a single. This keeps the scoreboard ticking over and equally is very frustrating to the bowler. This approach creates a very positive frame of mind. Too many batsmen take a negative outlook in the middle, which can lead to dismissal.

It is amazing how many cricketers get out in the 20s and 30s. They start with the right intentions – get to 10 then 20 by picking up ones and twos and hitting the bad balls for fours. Then they relax and are out. Perhaps there has been a change in bowlers or spin has been introduced, either way they lose concentration.

The batsman should maintain the game plan and focus with which they started the innings. Big hundreds are the target.

Set goals. The batsman must keep driving towards those goals. This will help them to maintain their concentration levels and create a hunger to score heavily and avoid the frustration of low scores.

Every batsman's dream should be a day with off-break bowlers.
ARTHUR MAILEY, THE AUSTRALIAN LEG-SPINNER IN HIS BOOK 10 FOR 66 AND ALL
THAT, 1959

The batting order

Balancing a batting order

For the team to function and prosper during the season, a balanced batting order is essential. There should be at least two or three players who are capable of batting through the innings and getting the side out of any difficult situations. If there are too many shot makers, then collapses are often likely as no one digs in; a team has to earn the right to allow their stroke-makers to play their natural game.

In an ideal world, two or three of a team's top seven batsmen would be all-rounders. This allows the team more batting-depth. Many teams have bowlers batting from No. 8 downwards who are effectively four No. 11s. This can put added pressure on the top seven, and lead to late order collapses.

Another key component for a successful team is the ability to develop big partnerships. Batsmen should look to work as a pair, set targets, bounce off each other and help each other through, not leave it to somebody else to get the runs.

The batting-order itself

All young cricketers who show talent with the bat should explore batting in a number of different positions between No. 1 and No. 6. Each batting position requires a different skill-set, so to help the batsman develop and give them a more rounded knowledge of the game they shouldn't get pigeon-holed in any one particular position too early in their development.

The following role descriptions apply to declaration cricket. One-day and Twenty20 cricket will be covered later in the book.

Opening the batting – No. 1 & No. 2

The opener's role is to see off the new ball attack and set the foundations for a good score. Opening batsmen should have excellent concentration and a sound defensive technique, and as a batsman moves up the age groups the ability to deal with fast, short-pitched deliveries is important.

Opening batsmen have traditionally been seen as defensive, but in the modern game it has become important for openers to look to score runs whenever the opportunity arises. Opening bowlers normally start with attacking fields, leaving plenty of chances for boundaries. Opening batsmen should be competent at the square cut and pull or hook shots as, with a hard new ball, a number of deliveries faced will be on the short side.

One of the two opening batsmen should aim to bat through the innings; this will allow the middle-order stroke players to play their natural game. It's crucial to encourage the importance of the partnership to both players. Some opening batsmen might even see their opening partnership as another way of contributing to the team – they may only make 20, but if the partnership makes 50 or more then they have not failed the team.

There are many different types of openers in Test cricket, as variable in technique and approach to their roles as the pragmatic Alastair Cook and the explosive Virender Sehwag. One thing unites the great openers – a decisiveness in defence or attack that lets the opening bowler know they are no pushover.

The top-order (No. 3 and No. 4)

The top-order batters are often regarded as the best two players in the team. Much of this is down to the versatility demanded of those batting at first or second drop – depending on when the first wickets fall they could be batting inside the first couple of overs, thus adopting a similar role to the opening batsmen, or batting when a solid foundation has been made and a more positive approach is necessary. Both players will have the ability to play fast bowling and spin, while ideally they should also have the ability and the confidence to dictate the tempo of the innings.

Whether the best player in the team should bat at No. 3 or No. 4 has always been a point of debate. Batting at No. 3 is arguably more important, because losing two early wickets can seriously damage a team's ambition. Consequently some sides prefer to play a better defensive player at No. 3 in order to shield their best player from the new ball for as long as possible. Rahul Dravid and Sachin Tendulkar for India are a good example of this, with contrasting strengths similar to a comedy double act, just without the laughs for opposition bowlers. Others, such as the former Australian captain Ricky Ponting, thrive on the responsibility that batting at No. 3 brings, and relish getting at the opposition as aggressively as the situation allows.

A team with a settled, productive top-order stands a good chance of being successful.

The middle-order (Nos. 5, 6 and 7)

Middle-order batsmen tend to be renowned for their attacking nature against pace and spin bowlers. Generally they bat when the ball is older and softer, and the fielding side is not as fresh. While these batsmen may not be as tight technically as the opening batsmen and may struggle against the new hard ball, they can be the difference between an average and a good score, so they should have a wide range of shots at their disposal and look to score.

Positivity is again important, as well as the ability to adapt their approach as the situation requires.

Is the team in trouble? In which case the middle-order need to dig in, and counter-attack selectively.

Are the team looking to increase the run rate? Then the middle-order players, knowing there are batsmen below them, may have to put the needs of the team before their own average and take more risks.

Iain O'Brien on being an effective tail-ender

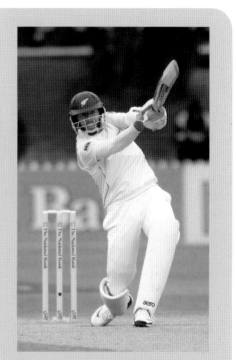

I batted for the guy at the other end, I batted for the partnership, and if I didn't get out we would score runs as a partnership. I always knew that, but it was just a question of learning how not to get out.

I didn't really work out how to bat for quite a long time. I got out a lot by being scared, playing short-balls when I shouldn't have done. I was pulling instead of ducking, because I didn't know what to do and the ball was going straight up in the air.

I did a lot of short ball work, and got a lot of confidence from learning how to duck and not get hit. I also vowed to never show the bowler fear. If I got knocked over I just got back up and stared back at them. The word that I used to myself when I was batting was courage, but I used the last four letters of that most of all. I learnt to channel and control the RAGE.

Iain O'Brien averaged 7.55 in 22 Tests for New Zealand between 2005 and 2009

It's very rewarding being a pain in the arse.
Jack Russell, England wicket-keeper, after saving the Johannesburg Test
with Mike Atherton in 1995

Lower middle-order (No. 8 and No. 9)

Could be the two all-rounders in the side. The lower middle-order tend to be hard hitting, attacking players whose role is to score quickly, or stay with the established batsmen as the situation dictates. If a batsman finds themselves batting at No. 8 or No. 9, the chances are they could be either a couple of places too high or too low. If they're too high, they will need to work as hard as they can to stay there. If they're too low, they should practise like a demon and use the chances they do get to show the coach and captain they should be higher up the order.

The tail-enders (No. 10 and No. 11)

Their roles are to give the strike to whichever lower order batsman they are in with. They are not renowned for their batting skills but still have important roles to play within the side. Rather than look at their individual batting averages, change their approach. Their partnerships become their average.

Gone are the days when teams could afford to carry four proper tail-enders, and opposition attacks don't go easy on tail-enders either. The higher level a cricketer plays at, the more they will be required to show willingness to learn and improve in other disciplines.

Remember: There's a great template for all tail-enders to follow. Mark Richardson was a left-arm spinner in New Zealand domestic cricket who batted firmly at No. 11. One day he got the yips, but was determined that it would not end his career, so taught himself batting. Richardson ended up opening in 38 consecutive Tests for New Zealand, ending with an average of 44.77 and four centuries including one at Lord's.

LIMITED-OVERS BATTING

4.

INTRODUCTION

Limited-overs cricket is all geared towards the batsman. In the professional game the public want to see runs and big hits, and this has manifested itself recently in the form of Twenty20 cricket.

This means there's a lot of fun to be had in limited-overs cricket in terms of run-scoring and experimenting with technique and stroke-play. Don't be fooled into thinking that limited-overs cricket is only for the big-hitters. Many of the most effective batsmen in one-day cricket are orthodox batsmen. Mahela Jayawardene, one of the most elegant stroke-players in the game, scored a hundred in the final of the 2011 World Cup, while at the time of going to press the ultra-orthodox Sachin Tendulkar is one of only two men to have hit a one-day double century. The other, inevitably, is Virender Sehwag.

The key to one-day cricket is for the batsman to know their own game, work out their scoring areas and stick to them. The rest is detail. It is important for a batsman to pick up their scoring-rate from declaration cricket, but that's easily done by picking up as many ones and twos as possible to complement the boundaries.

With the advent of Twenty20 cricket, limited-over formats have become an increasingly influential part of the modern game.

Games tend to be in two main formats:
- **Twenty20** – 20 overs a side.
- **Traditional limited-overs** – single innings games normally lasting 40, 45 or 50 overs per innings.

Naturally the shorter the game, the more emphasis is placed on attacking stroke play.

The singles and the threes are the vital scoring shots in cricket, not the twos and the fours.

Bobby Simpson, Australian captain, on the advantages to batsmen of rotating the strike

Key points for batting in limited-overs

The batsman should try to:

- Score off every ball; remember each delivery has a number – 6, 4, 3, 2, 1. Try not to let the bowling side bowl dots, be positive.
- See every ball as an event.
- Understand their role within the team and in the situation.
- Always look to run well between the wickets.
- Target the first ball of an over for boundaries to put pressure on the bowler.

Batting in long-form (50-over) cricket

It's easiest to break batting down into stages in 50-overs cricket.

Depending on the rules of the format, the opposition might have to observe power-plays (when only two fielders are allowed outside the 30-yard circle), and keep a certain number of fielders within the 30-yard circle at all times. While the pressure is on to score quickly while the field is up, the batsman should remember that they can often achieve this by placing the ball well with orthodox shots.

First 15 overs

- Play straight and focus on hitting in the V.
- Set the platform to attack later in the innings.
- One of the players who would typically bat in the first 15-overs (the openers, No. 3 and No. 4) should set themselves to bat through the innings, and give other batsmen someone to bat around.
- Once the batsman is in and feels comfortable with the pace and bounce of the wicket, they can be more expansive.
- Fielding restrictions should mean there are plenty of scoring opportunities and gaps in the field to exploit without being rash.
- If the pitch is relatively flat, a side may want to put a pinch-hitter at the top of the order. A pinch-hitter is a lower-order aggressive batsman who has been promoted to open the innings with the sole purpose of being destructive. Equally, if the pace of the innings becomes too slow, the pinch-hitter can be introduced at any time in the innings. When looking for a potential pinch-hitter, choose someone who strikes the ball cleanly and has the ability to hit straight over the bowler's head.

The middle overs (16–40)

- Fields are often set deep protecting the boundaries, this allows plenty of opportunity to pick up ones and twos.
- Ones and twos will bring the field in, allowing bigger shots to be played.
- Develop partnerships and keep wickets in hand.

The death (overs 40–50)

- A team should aim to have at least one 'in' batsman going into the death.
- This player should aim to bat through this period – two new batsmen leads to difficulty in maintaining a healthy scoring rate and can result in collapses.
- Look to score off every ball. Six runs an over is the bare minimum at this stage.
- Try to hit a boundary off the first ball of the over. This puts added pressure on the bowlers and can force them into mistakes.
- Try to study a bowler through the innings. If they bowl slower balls, try to learn to pick them. If they are trying to bowl yorkers and the keeper is standing back, the batsman can move out of their crease to disrupt the bowler's length.

Chasing down a total

Chasing a total is often more difficult than setting one because, when the game gets close, batsmen have to deal with their own nerves as well as the pressure to score runs. There are several things the batting side can do to make it easier:

- Look for one of the top four to bat through.
- Break the chase up into smaller targets, e.g. 50 off 10 overs.
- Aim to keep a good tempo or scoring-rate.
- Look to rotate strike.
- Openers should be positive but not reckless.
- Keep wickets in hand.
- Be patient, the odd maiden or slow scoring over is not a disaster.
- Don't leave it to others. If a batsman is in, they must try to see it home. It's a lot more difficult to hit boundaries for a batsman who is new to the crease.
- Keep composure under pressure. Don't be hurried. The batsman should try to find a routine before each ball that helps them keep calm.
- When working out required run-rate, the team should discount the last over so they are aiming to win in the 49th over.

Kieran Powell on building an innings in one-day cricket

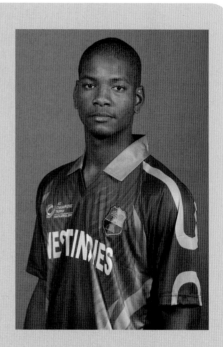

I like to hit an early boundary and then get off strike after that. That gives confidence and the innings flows from there. As you get set in, the field spreads and gaps become easier to hit; you'll start being the one dictating the terms to the opposition. After you gain control you must know when to attack and when to just go with the pace of the game. I generally have the same mindset in one-day cricket as declaration as I'm looking to score at any given opportunity. The difference is after the fielding restrictions are lifted in one day international cricket. Then it becomes very easy to get singles, and balls that you'd leave in a Test you'll look to score off. I look to keep the run rate at five or as close to five for the majority of the innings. This gives a good platform for the last 10 overs to set up a good score.

Kieran Powell plays Test and one-day cricket for West Indies. He played under Mark Davis at Millfield School

I don't think that it's just a young man's game at all. You just can't go out there and smash every ball possible, you need someone in the team to actually neutralise the innings. You have seen Rahul Dravid playing so many great knocks for us, you need to use brains as well in IPL to build your innings.
VIRAT KOHLI SAYS TWENTY20 IS NOT JUST A YOUNG MAN'S GAME, 2010

Twenty20

Twenty20 is by nature a more frenetic version of the game. There are fewer balls to score in, so each one is more important. Many of these principles are also applicable to the death overs of the 50-over game. In Twenty20 the majority of matches are decided by the power-play overs and the death overs. The side that wins both normally wins the match.

- Each ball is an event; look to score off every ball – rotate the strike.
- Try and make sure the bigger hitters in the team get most of the strike.
- The pressure to score off every ball gives batsmen more of a licence to improvise and be innovative. A confident batsman should look to manipulate the field and create boundary opportunities in their stronger scoring areas.
- Don't over-complicate. The batsman should play shots they are confident with, and identify the best areas to try and hit through.
- Disrupt the bowler – bat outside the crease and deep in the crease to take advantage of the length they are bowling.
- Move from side to side. For example, a slight left leg clearance can free up the arms to attack.
- Play smart cricket. Look to hit boundaries but still pick up ones and twos when it's not possible to play big shots. Twenty overs is still a long time – the team won't last long if batsmen slog mindlessly from the start.
- However much the batsman is moving around the crease, they should aim to keep their head still when the bowler releases to maximise power and timing.
- Retain composure under pressure.

Suresh Raina on batting in Twenty20 cricket

Back your instinct

Twenty20 is a great format. When you are chasing 180 or so, it's a real battle between batsman and bowler – who is going to get nervous first?

The most important thing is you have to back your instinct. You know your own game and you have to know when the right time is to take a chance. Twenty20 is all about your mindset.

Don't worry about getting out, if you are playing an aggressive stroke go right through with it, and that gives you the best chance of a good result.

Dominate the bowler

If you get a chance to score a boundary first ball, go for it. Cricket, and particularly Twenty20, is all about how you dominate your opposition on the field. It is about your approach, your intensity and your body-language. You need to be up all the time whether you are fielding, bowling or batting.

Identify your hitting areas

You need to know your strong areas and where there are fielders that you have to clear. I don't play any shots pre-planned. I follow the bowler. If he bowls short at me, I make sure I can move between front foot and back foot. It's a process – whatever you do in practice you have to do in the match. In the last four overs, when you are trying to smash everything, that might change.

Innovation

Play straight initially, and focus on orthodox cricket shots. If you look at Jacques Kallis as an example, the ones scoring the runs in the IPL are using proper cricket strokes, and you can learn from the big players. You can't just smash every ball. You have to play cricketing strokes too.

If you do have the ability to innovate like Eoin Morgan and Tillekeratne Dilshan, then play those shots when you have really got yourself in, past fifty or so. It spreads the field out and gives more room for ones and twos.

Suresh Raina plays Test, one-day and Twenty20 cricket for India. This interview originally appeared in the Wisden Cricketer

THE MENTAL SIDE OF BATTING

5.

> There is probably a greater premium on temperament for a batsman
> than for any player in any branch of sport.
> SIR DONALD BRADMAN, THE ART OF CRICKET, 1958

INTRODUCTION

Over years of coaching we are now seeing more and more boys struggling with the mental side of the game. Why is that? There is no simple answer. Maybe it's the pressure to perform. Maybe it's external pressures, maybe it's the increased demand for results across young children's lives now.

There is a constant fear of getting out, a developing culture of reluctance to take risks. It would be great if coaches could get them all to take that freedom of net practice and winter work out to the middle.

This doesn't just apply to schoolboys, it's equally prevalent to cricketers of all levels. The advice below can only be general, but read it carefully.

Coping with failure

Loss of form is one of the most difficult things for any batsman to deal with. Every batsman must deal with a run of low scores, but they must try to make sure it doesn't become a cyclical process – loss of confidence leading to poor decision making and more low scores. Stay calm and try to retain self-belief – here are some basic rules to follow to try to get the runs flowing again.

- The harder the batsman tries the worse it gets. The batsman should note what they have done wrong, but not be overly self-critical.
- Loss of form happens to every player; it is how the player deals with the situation that is important.
- Get to 20 in singles – play no expansive shots.
- The batsman should identify their best two or three shots and stick to them.

- Go back to basics – check grip/stance/pick-up.
- Keep the ball close to the body at all times. Don't go searching for it away from the body.
- Play in the 'V'. Stick to the straight-batted strokes rather than cross-batted ones.
- Hit some tennis balls to build up confidence.
- Often the problem is mental. Don't fear failure. The batsman should make a list of their best shots, remember their best innings and change negative thoughts to positive ones.

Michael Vaughan on learning to separate batting from captaincy

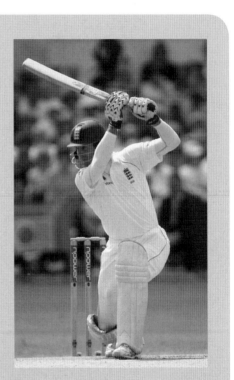

Coping with failure is probably the hardest thing for a captain. Sitting at the end of the game when your team has lost and you haven't scored runs is horrible, but it's life, you're never going to succeed every time. As long as you can have your different hats on, your captaincy hat when you're in the field, and your batting hat when you're in the middle then you'll be OK. Sometimes in my captaincy, not often fortunately, I couldn't do that. The ones that struggle take their captaincy out to bat and batting out to captain. You have to be able to define each job, but you can't take things too seriously. It's still just a game of cricket.

Michael Vaughan captained England in 51 Tests between 2003 and 2008. This interview originally appeared in the Wisden Cricketer

Changing your thought process

There are simple ways for a batsman who is low on confidence to change the way they think about their batting.

- To be consistently successful, the batsman should believe that they are capable of meeting the challenges and demands set before them.
- They should know that the training that they have done is more than sufficient for them to succeed.
- They should try to maintain high levels of self-belief throughout.

To avoid negative thoughts and personal doubts of their ability, the batsman should create a personal list of positive statements that specifically apply to them. Examples below:

- I can perform well under pressure.
- I feel mentally tough.
- I have trained well and am well prepared.
- I am ready for tough situations.
- I feel confident with my game.
- I believe I can achieve anything.

The batsman should repeat these regularly, select an up-to-date list and place it in their cricket bag. They should read it on occasions when they may feel stressed or negative about their game.

Change from negative self-talk to positive self-talk

How to change self-talk

Negative opening

I can't ... I'm worried ... If only ... I hope ... It's difficult ...

Positive opening

I can if ... I'll be fine if ... When ... It is a challenge ...

Negative

I'm worried about facing that quick opening bowler.

That umpire has probably cost us the game.

I can't get that mistake out of my mind.

Coping with success

Sometimes batsmen even have to learn to cope with all their success. Strange as it may seem, too much success can sometimes be as damaging to a player's game as failure. Over-confidence can lead to poor shot selection and technical flaws creeping into their game. Batsmen should enjoy the good times, but make sure they stick to the routines and drills that got them there.

- Savour and enjoy the good days.
- Be humble.
- Try to stay on a level plain with good and bad days.
- Batsmen should log dropped catches in their innings, and where they were dropped, and try to pre-empt their luck running out.

Justin Langer on batting

How important is concentration for a young batsman?

Concentration is important for all players regardless of their age. Without concentration, the chances of surviving the next ball diminish. If you don't survive the next ball, you are no longer in the game because you are sitting in the changing room feeling sorry for yourself. Players who marry a sound technique with a strong mind (concentrated mind) become difficult to dismiss and if you are still in, you are still in the game and able to make a difference to the result.

What techniques would you recommend to a young player to keep their concentration in the middle?

My pre-ball routine was critical to my ability to score runs. This allows you to be comfortable and ready for the next ball that is bowled to you. Mental toughness is concentration, and concentration is having the ability to give 100% attention to the next ball bowled to you. This takes practice and is without doubt a learned skill; just like learning the pull shot or cover drive.

What drills you would recommend to a young player to help them improve their concentration?

Practise seeing the ball out of the bowler's hand. This sounds simple but it is actually quite difficult unless you practise it over and over and over again. You can also practice seeing the ball as late as you can. I used to practise this by seeing the seam of the ball or the dimples on the bowling machine balls. If you watch the ball closely and stay balanced and still, you can definitely practise seeing the seam or the dimples. Start slow and then increase the pace as you get better at it. For the older player meditation is a great technique and also understanding how distractions on and off the field can lead to a less concentrated and focused mind.

What would be the three main pieces of advice you would give to any young batter?

1. **Love** batting. If you love to bat then practice will be fun. The more you practise the better you will get, and the better you get the more you will want to practise. Without practice and passion you have no chance of being a really good player.
2. Understand that peak performance is a synergy between having a good **technique**, a strong **mind**, a fit **body** and a balanced and happy **spirit**. You have to work on all of these areas to be a good player.
3. **Watch the ball like a hawk.** The only thing standing in the way of success and failure for a batsman is the ball. Watch it like a hawk from the moment it leaves the bowler's hand to the moment it hits the middle of your bat.

Justin Langer played 105 Tests for Australia between 1993 and 2007

PRACTICE, PRACTICE, PRACTICE

6.

Enjoyment, given and felt, is the chief thing about Compton's batting. It is a clear-flowing stream, a breath of half-holiday among work days.
R.C. Robertson-Glasgow on Denis Compton

INTRODUCTION

A cricketer can read this book as many times as they like, but if they don't put in the hours by themselves or in the nets practising the skills they've read about, they'll never make a batsman.

Practice should never be a drag. As Justin Langer said earlier in the book, *love* batting. That extends to time in the nets as well in the middle. A batsman should work hard on their own faults, be self-aware but never overly self-critical.

It's important to put the work in, but don't over-practise. Practising the same skill for a prolonged period of time might exhaust certain muscles. If a player is practising tired then they may be teaching themselves bad habits. A player should listen to their body.

Fitness

Fitness and strength are important for the young cricketer. If a batsman plans on spending some time in the middle they're going to have to be fit. There's no point in a batsman concentrating hard for a couple of hours, only to throw it away when they're in the 80s because they're tired and they've lost concentration.

Every cricketer has different fitness needs. We recommend a player speaks to their coach, or somebody at their local gym, to help them work out a fitness programme that suits them personally.

PLANNING YOUR WINTER AND SUMMER

If a player doesn't have access to a local school or county coach, then it's worth them going down to their local club to see if there's one who can help. It is important to formulate a plan for winter development. This should begin with a chat about how the summer went. From this the player can work out what areas they need to develop during the winter.

All batsmen should keep a diary and write their interpretation of their coaching sessions, diet and fitness routine. During the cricket season they should record runs scored, wickets taken and how they got out, or which type of bowler took their wicket each time. From this they may find a common denominator to work on in their winter training programme.

Each month a review with the team coach is a must — has the batsman mastered what they set out to do? What do they want to work on next, e.g. set-up/triggers to pace/pressing to spin? These things can take a long time to address. Remember fitness and fielding are equally important. In the modern game a cricketer should look to become a specialist in the field as well as in their other chosen discipline.

Net practice

When the player's winter technical work is well under way, it is useful to have the occasional net session to see if the initial changes are successful. Early winter (before Christmas for UK summer) nets serve little or no purpose if a player is making changes to their game. Nets merely reinforce faults.

- The batsman should step away or work solely on their skills with hitting off cones, bobble-feeds, throw downs and the bowling machine. **Two months before the season starts** is the time to start netting regularly to get used to timing trigger movements and monitoring how successful any changes have become (possibly use a video camera).
- Once the player is comfortable with the above it is then appropriate to introduce scenarios to net sessions. Discuss with the bowler a match situation. The bowler sets the field; after three overs discuss how it went. The batsman may want to work on sweeping the spinners or rotating the strike — whatever they want to develop, they should not forget to discuss these with the coach and bowlers prior to the net.
- Some players find netting hard to concentrate in and just go through the motions. A way of changing this is once every three net sessions, if the batsman is out, then out of the nets he comes. It is amazing how this changes their approach and concentration to the net session.

Using the bowling machine

The bowling machine is an ideal model for shot grooving and specific skill practice. If a batsman doesn't already have access to one on occasion, it's worth asking at a school or local club as they are invaluable practice aids. The bowling machine offers:

- Extreme practice conditions for the elite performer facing high pace intensity or swing.
- The chance to work on a specific fault as more balls can be faced than conventional throw downs, and with greater accuracy.
- Shot grooving.
- Automatic feed – the ability to practise alone.
- Electronic random delivery mode – ball speed changes by 5mph each delivery creating a more general net practice.
- The chance to practise against short deliveries using glow balls (softer than normal machine balls) building up the batsman's confidence without the fear of getting hurt.
- Can be moved on to grass wickets during the season, where spin settings can be used on worn out surfaces.

Remember: A player should be careful when they're using a bowling machine, never walk in front of it when there is a chance it might be about to deliver a ball. Equally, the batsman shouldn't be too ambitious when facing one. Bowling machines can bowl balls up to 90mph, but it's best for a batsman to start slow and work up through the speeds.

THE FUTURE

Cricketers who aspire to either go and play professional cricket or reach their highest possible level are increasingly becoming aware of the needs of the modern player. Professional counties demand two or three-dimensional players – fitness and fielding are as important as batting and bowling, while diet and nutrition are now key components for every player.

All cricketers with ambitions of playing regularly should join their local cricket team if they haven't already done so. If you are a younger player you should look for a thriving youth section and active coaches within the club. Are young players being integrated into the senior sides? Is it a multi-sports facility where perhaps the whole family can join and enjoy all the facilities? Encourage your friends to attend. You could then get a group to practise together during the evenings and school holidays.

If you are an older player you should look for a club with a good net culture, and teams for a range of abilities.

ADVICE FOR COACHES

There are two types of coach: a discovery coach and a tell coach.

The discovery coach allows the batsmen to explore options. Each player is unique and individual, and although the basic techniques should be adhered to, it's great for inexperienced players to show flair, initiative to excite, to challenge and to discuss.

A coach can hope to give his players a complete understanding of their game, be it technical, tactical, physical or mental, and to realise their full potential before they leave. Whether you play at international, county, club or social level, enjoyment is the priority and your game will certainly be enhanced if you enjoy it.

Coaching sessions should be relaxed – a coach should try to make sure that the players believe that they are most important. A coach has to earn their trust and respect, it is then that the relationship between coach/student can really flourish. Encouragement is important but it's also a good idea to constantly challenge pupils to get out of their comfort zone for them to improve their game.

A really enjoyable aspect of coaching is problem-solving. Some coaches look for things that simply aren't there just to justify their existence, but it is equally important on occasions to say nothing except well played. It can give a coach huge satisfaction when major/minor changes can make such a difference and improve the individual game.

Some boys and players struggle when moving school or club – they get big fish/small pond syndrome so they may drift away from the game due to fear of failure and not being centre of attention like they were in their previous school or club. The key to success is to embrace all challenges, have an open mind and be able to discuss things with someone.

Player and coach relationship
What the coach should remember
- Allow the pupil to become independent but be able to discuss things openly.
- Coaching is not about the pupil hanging on the coach's every word.
- Don't over coach. You are educating the player to think for themselves while maintaining a close working relationship with the coach.

- You should be encouraging the player to explore all avenues of their game, and find out what works for them.

What the player should remember
- Enjoy the game.
- The coach is there to help you fulfil your potential and stretch you to the limits.
- Treat the coach with the respect you would like to be treated.

APPENDIX

MODES OF DISMISSAL

1. Caught: When the ball is caught on the full by a member of the fielding side after it has touched the batsman's bat, or the batsman's glove while their hand is on the bat.

2. Bowled: When the ball is bowled to the striking batsman and dislodges the bails from the stumps at the striker's end.

3. Leg before wicket (LBW): The LBW rule is complex, so we've included the whole law.

   The striker is out LBW in the circumstances set out below:

   (a) The bowler delivers a ball, not being a no ball and

   (b) the ball, if it is not intercepted full pitch, pitches in line between wicket and wicket or on the off-side of the striker's wicket and

   (c) the ball not having previously touched their bat, the striker intercepts the ball, either full pitch or after pitching, with any part of their person and

   (d) the point of impact, even if above the level of the bails, either (i) is between wicket and wicket or (ii) if the striker has made no genuine attempt to play the ball with their bat, is either between wicket and wicket or outside the line of the off stump and

   (e) but for the interception, the ball would have hit the wicket.

4. Run out: When a fielder, bowler or wicket-keeper removes one or both of the bails with the ball by hitting the stumps when a batsman is out of their ground attempting a run. If the bails have been removed, then the fielding side can remove a stump from the ground and as long as it is in contact with the ball the batsman is still run out.

5. Stumped: When the wicket-keeper removes the bails while the striking batsman is out of his crease. This sort of dismissal will occur when the wicket-keeper is standing up to the stumps.

6. Hit wicket: When the striking batsman dislodges the bails during or in the immediate aftermath of a delivery.

7. Handled the ball: When the batsman deliberately handles the ball without the permission of the fielding team.

8. Hit the ball twice: When the batsman deliberately strikes the ball a second time, except for the sole purpose of guarding his wicket.

9. Obstructing the field: When a batsman deliberately stops a fielder from attempting to field the ball, or throw at the stumps.

10. Timed out: When a new batsman takes more than three minutes to take their position in the field to replace a dismissed batsman. (If the delay is protracted, the umpires may cause the match to be forfeited.)

Miscellany

A batsman can leave the field without being dismissed if they are injured or ill. The batsman is not out; they may return to bat later in the same innings if sufficiently recovered. Also, an unimpaired batsman may retire, in which case they are treated as being dismissed retired out.

An individual cannot be out — 'bowled', 'caught', 'leg before wicket', 'stumped', or 'hit wicket' – off a no ball.

The batsman who is not on strike may be run out by the bowler if they leave their crease before the bowler bowls, and a batsman can be out obstructing the field or retired out at any time. Timed out by its nature is a dismissal without a delivery. With all other modes of dismissal, only one batsman can be dismissed per ball bowled. Obstructing the field, handled the ball, timed out and hit the ball twice dismissals are extremely rare.

MISCELLANEOUS

The following taken from the MCC's *Laws of Cricket*. Please refer to the laws in full for a complete explanation.

The no-ball rule

1. **Mode of delivery**

   (a) The umpire shall ascertain whether the bowler intends to bowl right handed or left handed, over or round the wicket, and shall so inform the striker. It is unfair if the bowler fails to notify the umpire of a change in his mode of delivery. In this case the umpire shall call and signal No ball.

   (b) Underarm bowling shall not be permitted except by special agreement before the match.

2. **Fair delivery – the arm**

   For a delivery to be fair in respect of the arm the ball must not be thrown. See 3 below. Although it is the primary responsibility of the striker's end umpire to assess the fairness of a delivery in this respect, there is nothing in this Law to debar the bowler's end umpire from calling and signalling No ball if he considers that the ball has been thrown.

(a) If, in the opinion of either umpire, the ball has been thrown, he shall call and signal No ball and, when the ball is dead, inform the other umpire of the reason for the call. The bowler's end umpire shall then

  (i) caution the bowler. This caution shall apply throughout the innings.

  (ii) inform the captain of the fielding side of the reason for this action.

  (iii) inform the batsmen at the wicket of what has occurred.

(b) If, after such caution, either umpire considers that, in that innings, a further delivery by the same bowler is thrown, the procedure set out in (a) above shall be repeated, indicating to the bowler that this is a final warning. This warning shall also apply throughout the innings.

(c) If either umpire considers that, in that innings, a further delivery by the same bowler is thrown, he shall call and signal No ball and when the ball is dead inform the other umpire of the reason for the call. The bowler's end umpire shall then

  (i) direct the captain of the fielding side to suspend the bowler forthwith. The over shall, if applicable, be completed by another bowler, who shall neither have bowled the previous over or part thereof nor be allowed to bowl any part of the next over. The bowler thus suspended shall not bowl again in that innings.

  (ii) inform the batsmen at the wicket and, as soon as practicable, the captain of the batting side of the occurrence.

(d) The umpires together shall report the occurrence as soon as possible after the match to the Executive of the fielding side and to any Governing Body responsible for the match, who shall take such action as is considered appropriate against the captain and the bowler concerned.

3. **Definition of fair delivery – the arm**

A ball is fairly delivered in respect of the arm if, once the bowler's arm has reached the level of the shoulder in the delivery swing, the elbow joint is not straightened partially or completely from that point until the ball has left the hand. This definition shall not debar a bowler from flexing or rotating the wrist in the delivery swing.

4. **Bowler throwing towards striker's end before delivery**

If the bowler throws the ball towards the striker's end before entering his delivery stride, either umpire shall call and signal No ball. See Law 42.16 (Batsmen stealing a run). However, the procedure stated in 2 above of caution, informing, final warning, action against the bowler and reporting shall not apply.

5. **Fair delivery – the feet**

For a delivery to be fair in respect of the feet, in the delivery stride

(a) the bowler's back foot must land within and not touching the return crease appertaining to his stated mode of delivery.

(b) the bowler's front foot must land with some part of the foot, whether grounded or raised

    (i)   on the same side of the imaginary line joining the two middle stumps as the return crease described in (a) above and

    (ii)   behind the popping crease.

If the bowler's end umpire is not satisfied that all of these three conditions have been met, he shall call and signal No ball.

6. **Ball bouncing more than twice or rolling along the ground**

The umpire shall call and signal No ball if a ball which he considers to have been delivered, without having previously touched bat or person of the striker, either

    (i)   bounces more than twice or

    (ii)   rolls along the ground before it reaches the popping crease.

7. **Ball coming to rest in front of striker's wicket**

If a ball delivered by the bowler comes to rest in front of the line of the striker's wicket, without having previously touched the bat or person of the striker, the umpire shall call and signal No ball and immediately call and signal Dead ball.

8. **Call of No ball for infringement of other Laws**

In addition to the instances above, No ball is to be called and signalled as required by the following Laws.

Law 40.3 – Position of wicket-keeper

Law 41.5 – Limitation of on side fielders

Law 41.6 – Fielders not to encroach on pitch

Law 42.6 – Dangerous and unfair bowling

Law 42.7 – Dangerous and unfair bowling - action by the umpire

Law 42.8 – Deliberate bowling of high full pitched balls

9. **Revoking a call of No ball**

An umpire shall revoke his call of No ball if the ball does not leave the bowler's hand for any reason.

10. **No ball to over-ride Wide**

A call of No ball shall over-ride the call of Wide ball at any time. See Laws 25.1 (Judging a Wide) and 25.3 (Call and signal of Wide ball).

11. Ball not dead

The ball does not become dead on the call of No ball.

12. Penalty for a No ball

A penalty of one run shall be awarded instantly on the call of No ball. Unless the call is revoked, the penalty shall stand even if a batsman is dismissed. It shall be in addition to any other runs scored, any boundary allowance and any other runs awarded for penalties.

13. Runs resulting from a No ball – how scored

The one run penalty shall be scored as a No ball extra. If other penalty runs have been awarded to either side these shall be scored as stated in Law 42.17 (Penalty runs). Any runs completed by the batsmen or any boundary allowance shall be credited to the striker if the ball has been struck by the bat; otherwise they shall also be scored as No ball extras. Apart from any award of 5 penalty runs, all runs resulting from a No ball, whether as No ball extras or credited to the striker, shall be debited against the bowler.

14. No ball not to count

A No ball shall not count as one of the over. See Law 22.3 (Validity of balls).

15. Out from a No ball

When No ball has been called, neither batsman shall be out under any of the Laws except 33 (Handled the ball), 34 (Hit the ball twice), 37 (Obstructing the field) or 38 (Run out).

The wide rule

1. Judging a Wide

(a) If the bowler bowls a ball, not being a No ball, the umpire shall adjudge it a Wide if, according to the definition in (b) below, in his opinion the ball passes wide of the striker where he is and which also would have passed wide of him standing in a normal guard position.

(b) The ball will be considered as passing wide of the striker unless it is sufficiently within his reach for him to be able to hit it with his bat by means of a normal cricket stroke.

2. Delivery not a Wide

The umpire shall not adjudge a delivery as being a Wide

(a) if the striker, by moving, either

    (i)   causes the ball to pass wide of him, as defined in 1(b) above or

(ii)   brings the ball sufficiently within his reach to be able to hit it by means of a normal cricket stroke.

(b) if the ball touches the striker's bat or person.

3. Call and signal of Wide ball

(a) If the umpire adjudges a delivery to be a Wide he shall call and signal Wide ball as soon as the ball passes the striker's wicket. It shall, however, be considered to have been a Wide from the instant of delivery, even though it cannot be called Wide until it passes the striker's wicket.

(b) The umpire shall revoke the call of Wide ball if there is then any contact between the ball and the striker's bat or person.

(c) The umpire shall revoke the call of Wide ball if a delivery is called a No ball. See Law 24.10 (No ball to over-ride Wide).

4. Ball not dead

The ball does not become dead on the call of Wide ball.

5. Penalty for a Wide

A penalty of one run shall be awarded instantly on the call of Wide ball. Unless the call is revoked (see 3(b) and (c) above), this penalty shall stand even if a batsman is dismissed, and shall be in addition to any other runs scored, any boundary allowance and any other runs awarded for penalties.

6. Runs resulting from a Wide - how scored

All runs completed by the batsmen or a boundary allowance, together with the penalty for the Wide, shall be scored as Wide balls. Apart from any award of 5 penalty runs, all runs resulting from a Wide shall be debited against the bowler.

7. Wide not to count

A Wide shall not count as one of the over. See Law 22.3 (Validity of balls).

8. Out from a Wide

When Wide ball has been called, neither batsman shall be out under any of the Laws except 33 (Handled the ball), 35 (Hit wicket), 37 (Obstructing the field), 38 (Run out) or 39 (Stumped).

ABOUT THE AUTHORS

ABOUT MARK DAVIS

Mark Davis was born in Kilve, West Somerset in 1962. A left-arm swing bowler, Mark played for Somerset between 1980 and 1987. During that time he opened the bowling with Ian Botham and Joel Garner. Other notable colleagues included Viv Richards, Martin Crowe and Vic Marks. Mark toured Zimbabwe with England 'A' in 1982, and after leaving the pro game he became a player-coach with Llangennech in the South Wales league, operating as a freelance coach in schools around Wiltshire, Dorset and Somerset. He joined Millfield as head coach in 1996, and has overseen the development of countless county players and a few international players since, as well as helping out at the Somerset academy. He has worked as an analyst on BBC Radio Bristol's cricket coverage since the early 1990s.

ABOUT SAM COLLINS

Sam Collins is a freelance cricket journalist and former editor of thewisdencricketer.com, who has previously worked for CricInfo and Guardian.co.uk.

Away from journalism Sam is a former Kent Under-19 opening bowler and captained Eton College in 2001. He still plays cricket when time allows.

AUTHORS' NOTE

The batsmen in this book were wearing helmets at all times when a ball was involved.

ACKNOWLEDGEMENTS

The authors would like to thank their partners Sophie and Kim for all their patience and help; Chris Greenwood, Andrew Roberts and Joseph Dale for translating Mark's scribbles; Christopher Gange and Jarrod Kimber for their assistance with photography; and Millfield School pupils for their participation and enthusiasm in all photo shoots. Many thanks to others; there are just too many to mention: this would not have been possible without your help.